A Teacher's Toolbox for Gifted Education

This book provides busy teachers with an adaptable toolbox of strategies for challenging gifted students that they can immediately put into practice in their classroom, school, or program. Chapters cover everything from makerspaces and project-based learning, to enrichment clubs, mentorships, creative thinking, and more. Each strategy includes an overview, resource guide, description of how it looks in the classroom, and all the information you need to put it into practice. With templates, charts, and links to videos illustrating the tools in action, *A Teacher's Toolbox for Gifted Education* is your go-to guide for creative ways to support advanced learners.

Todd Stanley is author of several teacher education books, including *Project-Based Learning for Gifted Students: A Handbook for the 21st-Century Classroom* (2nd edition), *How the Hell Do We Motivate These Kids?*, and *Promoting Rigor Through Higher-Level Questioning*.

A Teacher's Toolbox for Gifted Education

20 Strategies You Can Use Today to Challenge Gifted Students

Todd Stanley

Routledge
Taylor & Francis Group

NEW YORK AND LONDON

Cover image: Shutterstock

First published 2022
by Routledge
605 Third Avenue, New York, NY 10158

and by Routledge
2 Park Square, Milton Park, Abingdon, Oxon, OX14 4RN

Routledge is an imprint of the Taylor & Francis Group, an informa business

© 2022 Taylor & Francis

Library of Congress Cataloguing-in-Publication Data
A catalog record for this title has been requested

ISBN: 978-1-032-14514-3 (hbk)
ISBN: 978-1-646-32225-1 (pbk)
ISBN: 978-1-003-23857-7 (ebk)

DOI: 10.4324/9781003238577

Typeset in Palatino
by MPS Limited, Dehradun

Contents

Introduction – *The Secret Sauce for Teaching Gifted Students*

I have been working in gifted education for the past 25 years and the question I get asked the most, besides what the heck does a gifted coordinator do, is what is the secret to teaching gifted students? Because you bought this book, I am prepared to let you in on this valuable information only told to a select few; the secret to teaching gifted students is…just good teaching. Bam, I know, mind blown.

There *is* no secret way to teach gifted students, no magic dust you can find in the teacher's supply closet, no perfect online program that gets the most out of students. But there are good teaching strategies that challenge these students as they would challenge any student no matter what his or her ability.

Another secret I'm going to let you in on (if you stick around long enough I'll tell you what "your student is a joy to have in class" really means on the report card); these strategies are not just reserved for gifted students. These strategies work with all children, special education included. That is why when I give a workshop to teachers on gifted strategies, I make sure they know they will be able to use what they learned with all of their students should they choose. This is not an either/or situation. The strategies should be incorporated into your classroom as you see fit. You may have to scaffold or differentiate activities for certain students (both terms teachers throw around a lot in gifted education without actually knowing what they mean).

You might be asking yourself, why it is a gifted toolbox then? Because these are strategies that may work with all students, but particularly well with gifted students. I cannot tell you how many times teachers have said to me, "this student gets done with his work so quickly, I don't have anything else for him to do". This book will give you some ideas for what you can do for such students as well as meeting the needs of other gifted children who often times get overlooked or little attention because there are bigger problems in the classroom that seem more urgent.

If you feel you are not terribly equipped to work with these gifted kids, this is through no fault of your own. Most teaching programs at universities across the country give little to no attention to meeting the specific needs of gifted students. There is quite a lot of time spent on special education students and supporting their unique learning needs, but this ignores the fact that gifted students have unique needs as well. I think one of the biggest myths about gifted students is that if they don't get any attention, they will be just fine. After all, they can figure it out for themselves. Remember, no matter how intelligent they

DOI: 10.4324/9781003238577-101

might be, they need the support of good folks to show them how to learn, how to grow, how to challenge themselves.

This book is for those teachers who are given the gifted cluster or enrichment group and told to teach them differently, without being given much training on how to do so. This book is also for the regular classroom teacher who has a sprinkling of gifted students in her class. It always comes as a surprise to folks when I send out the list of gifted students in their classes. I get emails back with the message of "are you sure this kid is gifted" or "I thought all of the gifted students were in the gifted program"? But the one that I get the most is "what am I supposed to do with these students"? That is what this book will do; give you ideas for what you can do, both big and small, to offer enrichment to those students who are capable or interested.

How this book is organized is it presents 20 different strategies that you could put in your toolbox. One of my educational philosophies is that we all bring strengths to the profession of teaching and if we try to be something that we are not, it will show. There are teachers who are born lecturers and can enthrall and engage students with their woven tales. And there are those teachers who choose to lecture, and yet listening to them is akin to sitting in the dentist's chair only you don't get the relaxing music. The important thing is developing the awareness to know what sort of teacher you are, which can be tricky because sometimes we don't think we are a certain teacher and yet once we try it, we take to it quite well. Early in my teaching career I taught my social studies class just like the dozens of traditional teachers I had had in my own learning career. I did this because I didn't know any other way and was mediocre at best. Then when I discovered project-based learning (which is one of the strategies in this book), we were like two star-crossed lovers, complementing each other in every way. This was not a fling though, it took a lot of years of dating, trying things and failing, trying them again, and hopefully having some semblance of success. When I left the classroom 18 years into my teaching career to go to administration, I still had not perfected this strategy and if I thought I had, I would have been mistaken. The other part of why teaching is such a difficult profession is because we constantly have to adapt ourselves and change our methods in order to keep up with the kids. Any teacher worth their salt is modifying what they are doing and trying to get better at their chosen profession. That is why you are reading this book.

Another secret to share is you should not try to do all of the strategies in this book. Some will fit you, some will not. Most will feel uncomfortable at first but it is this discomfort where the most learning takes place. I would not do all 20 of the strategies, but I would choose some that maybe aren't exactly in your wheelhouse but could be with a little bit of work. It is not Harry Potter where if you skip a chapter or two you won't know what is going on with the story. It is not meant to be read from cover to cover. Find chapters that speak to your style of teaching and give them a try.

The 20 strategies in this book in no particular order are as follows:

- ◆ Bulletin board enrichment
- ◆ Enrichment clubs
- ◆ Higher level questioning
- ◆ Performance assessments
- ◆ Pre-assessment
- ◆ Independent projects

- Makerspace
- Students as teachers
- Four corners
- Project-based learning
- STEM design challenges
- Bonus opportunities
- Student choice
- Inquiry learning
- Differentiated centers
- Creative thinking
- Depth and Complexity
- 20time
- Board game enrichment
- Mentors/Mentorships

Each chapter gives an overview of the strategy, what it looks like in the classroom, where to find resources, what impact it will have on your teaching/classroom, and how much work it will require of you to successfully execute it.

I also will provide a rating that indicates how much impact this strategy will have on your day-to-day teaching. In other words, it it just something extra you have in your classroom as an opportunity for students to try, or it is the main pedagogy you are using while teaching. There are levels in between those as well. Here is what I call the impact on teaching scale:

1. It will require little to no change to day-to-day practices, act as additional opportunities for students to partake in outside of their main work.
2. It will require slight adjustments to your day, which could be anything from taking 15 minutes out of class to work on it or using it as a brain break. It is not however the main lesson, it is getting students warmed up for the main lesson or is extending it.
3. Might not be prevalent all of the time in the classroom but is used enough so that one would notice when it is being used. Has become so routine for students that little to no explanation needs to be given when students are doing it, rather they know what they should be doing from past experience.
4. This is a strategy that drives a lot of the learning but is mixed in with other forms of pedagogy as well. Students might only use this for certain topics or subject areas, but not others. When it is used, it is obvious to someone observing the class and the students know how to do it.
5. This is many times a different way of teaching. It is the main driver for how students are learning. When someone walks into your room, they can see the strategy in action constantly.

Keep in mind, some of the strategies can be different ratings depending on how you use it.

To help with this learning process, I have made video tutorials outlining each strategy known as Todd Talks. These show examples of what this strategy can look like and give further explanation. They are good for visual learners or if someone just needs to review.

These are all free and located on my YouTube channel under Gifted ToolBox https://www.youtube.com/watch?v=S9Kuxa_kR5w&list=PLI39aTw2zrCqYENF-GFlksPysneXUp-lQ.

All of the strategies I am going to share with you are ones that I field tested in my own classroom. I have taught everything from second graders to junior and seniors in high school, worked in pull-out, magnet, push-in (co-teaching), and cluster grouping models of gifted education, and taught all four core subject areas as well as gym and technology. Because of this, I have needed to use all sorts of strategies depending on the age and abilities of my students, how long I was going to have them for the day, and what I was teaching them. Even though I am now a gifted coordinator, I still make efforts to teach children rather than just working with adults (another secret, children are more fun and much easier). This comes in advising enrichment clubs, co-teaching with other teachers, guest teaching for some classes, teaching at gifted summer camps, and working with gifted students from China in a virtual setting. I know these strategies work because I used them firsthand. Hopefully, you will find similar success with them.

Bulletin Board Enrichment

Todd Talk Explaining the Strategy
https://youtu.be/S9Kuxa_kR5w [1]

Overview of the Strategy

As teachers, we have bulletins board spread throughout the classroom. What do we use them for? Some teachers put up student work, others have inspirational messages, others might post the classroom rules and procedures. What if we used them for enrichment purposes? What if students could go to the bulletin boards and find activities that allow them to explore their curiosity, to expand their thinking, or to challenge them. That is how bulletin board enrichment works. You have items set up at these bulletin boards that students can choose to do whenever there is downtime in the classroom.

What Does It Look Like in the Classroom?

Students are assigned some problems to do, or asked to complete a worksheet, or some other activity where the class as a whole is allotted a specific amount of time. There are always those few kids who get through the work in no time, leaving this awkward downtime where the student has to wait for everyone to catch up. Some of these students will pick up a book to bide their time, others might draw. Another group gets into trouble because they are bored and entertain themselves by distracting others or being mischievous, after all, you know what they say about idle hands. What if instead of having nothing to do, students have something productive they can choose to do?

A student walks up to one of the bulletin boards, grabs a paper provided, and works on some brain teasers. Another bulletin board has trivia questions that students either submit on a sticky note or a Google Form. A third bulletin board has book suggestions as well as a small shelf with books next to it. The student grabs one of these books and takes it back to her seat to read.

DOI: 10.4324/9781003238577-1

While these students are doing these enrichment activities, the other students who are still working are left uninterrupted to finish. They are not even aware that something else is going on around them. They also don't feel as though they have been left out of anything because these bulletin boards are still available for them tomorrow, or before class begins, or during indoor recess.

Your bulletin board enrichment can take whatever form you want to, as long as its purpose is to challenge the thinking of students. I had five bulletin boards spread around the room. Three of them were attached to the walls, the other two were just loose bulletin boards that I could place anywhere I wanted. At each of these bulletin boards were plenty of copies of the work students were challenged to do, or blank slips for them to put their answer on for a possible prize, or a synopsis of a book or two that was designed to create interest in reading it.

I generally had five categories for enrichment:

Useless trivia: This was just as the name sounds; trivia like you would find in Trivial Pursuit or on Jeopardy. They could be answered in a word or two. Because I was a social studies teacher, a lot of the questions had to do with history, geography, culture, or government. These were not however tied completely to my curriculum. I taught ancient history, and yet a lot of the questions I asked were more modern-day ones. Some examples of questions I asked students are given here:

♦ What is the only two US states to end in a letter that no other state does?
♦ What country did not give its women the right to vote until 1984?
♦ US schools typically take three months for summer break. How long does the typical Japanese school take?
♦ December 10 is Human Rights Day decreed by the United Nations. When was the United Nations created?
♦ What man served as president for a single day on March 3, 1849?

Even though finding the answers to these might be as easy as a Google search or asking Alexa, these questions were meant to ignite further curiosity in students. Trying to recall which state ends in a letter that none of the others do, you would really have to pause and think about it. You might think O but then you remember Idaho, Ohio, and Colorado. Or maybe you might think it is an I which is not common, but there are Hawaii, Mississippi, and Missouri. You finally land on New York or Wyoming, which are both correct, but they did not come immediately to mind, you had to think about it a little. When students research when the United Nations was created, hopefully they will learn what it is and what purpose it serves. They might even dive a little deeper to gain a better understanding. When students learn that David Rice Atchison served as the president for only a single day, they might want to research under what circumstances Atchison was in that required him to take the office.

You could tailor the questions to whatever subject area you teach. You could have math questions such as:

- What is the only even prime number?
- How many sides does a nonagon have?
- How many seconds are in one day?

Or ELA questions such as:

- What is the shortest complete sentence in the English language that consists of only one word?
- What is the longest word that has its letters in alphabetical order?
- What single word has 464 definitions to it?

Or just general interesting trivia:

- Approximately how many square miles of the earth are still left unexplored?
- Everyone knows to find a four leaf clover is good luck. What are the most leaves ever found on a clover?
- On a standard typing keyboard, which vowel is not on the top line of letters?

You hopefully get the point by now. The main idea is to have questions that would be interesting to students and would tap into the innate curiosity many of them possess.

Brain teasers: These cause students to think a little more than just a simple trivia question. They are designed to use higher level thinking skills in order to solve. The three types of brain teasers I offered to students were:

- Rebus puzzles: These are puzzles in which words are represented by a combination of pictures, letters, symbols, and so on. You have to try and guess the answer from the clues provided. For example, if the puzzle were to show this:

    Students would have to see the square and the word "think", and try to figure out how they fit together, coming up with a word or saying that is common vernacular. They would also have to determine what the positioning on the page has to do with it. The word "think" is not inside, but outside. Then their brain might figure out box is a synonym for square, and then come up with the answer of "think outside the box".

    There would be a worksheet full of these rebus puzzles, and students could get one and see how many of them they could get correct.

This is what one of the worksheets looked like:

♦ Riddles: The next sort of brain teasers were riddles meant to confound students and get them to think a little deeper. These were usually a sentence long. Here is an example of a riddle:

I'm tall when I'm young, and short when I'm old.

Students would read this and realize this is opposite of what usually occurs. People start short when they are babies, and grow much taller by the time they are old enough to be an adult. So it is not a person. What object then grows shorter the older it gets? They might try answers such as daylight which grows shorter the longer the day gets, a pencil that gets sharpened as it gets used more, or some other object that whittles down the longer it is used. Hopefully they will arrive at "a candle" that gets shorter the longer it burns.

Here are some other examples of riddles I have used with students:

1. What gets wetter and wetter the more it dries?
   • A towel
2. What can you catch but not throw?
   • A cold

3. The more of them you take, the more you leave behind?
   - Footsteps
4. The more you take away, the larger it becomes.
   - A hole
5. When one does not know what it is, then it is something. But when one knows what it is, it is nothing.
   - A riddle

I would have a worksheet with ten of these on it and students would try to see how many they could get.

- ◆ 3D puzzles: The final type of brain teaser I used was meant not only to challenge the mind, but to get students doing something tactile as well. I had a few of these available in case more than one student wanted to work on it. Some of the puzzles I had were as follows:
  - Rubik's Cube
  - Peg Game
  - Letter puzzle
  - ThinkFun Pocket Brain Teasers
  - 15 puzzle

Students could take these back to their desks and work on them at their leisure. If they got stuck, they were allowed to ask for a hint.

Book club: Just as it sounds, the book club involved students reading a book of the month posted at one of the bulletin boards. I based these books on a few criteria.

- ◆ A book I had previously read and knew was good
- ◆ A book students were reading and looked interesting to me
- ◆ A book that starts a series, meant to encourage further reading

I placed multiple copies of this book in a small library by the bulletin board, which students could borrow. I switched out the books every month, trying to rotate different interests. Here is an example of the books I posted one year:

- ◆ August/September – *The Lost Hero* (Rick Riordan)
- ◆ October – *The Selection* (Kiera Cass)
- ◆ November – *Ten Little Indians* (Agatha Christie)
- ◆ December – *The Book Thief* (Markus Zusak)
- ◆ January – *My Brother Sam Is Dead* (James and Christopher Collier)
- ◆ February – *Uglies* (Scott Westerfield)
- ◆ March – *The Mysterious Benedict Society* (Trenton Lee Stewart)
- ◆ April – *The Maze Runner* (James Dashner)
- ◆ May – *The Ruins of Gorlan* (John Flanagan)

The challenge, especially when working with middle school students, was finding a book that was above grade level and challenging for them, while at the same time being age appropriate. Even though my 5th graders could handle the reading level of a John Green book, I didn't want them reading about those teenage issues at such a young age. One solution to this is using classic books. They are typically appropriate for all ages, while at the same time having a high reading level. Authors such as Arthur Conan Doyle, H.G. Wells, Agatha Christie, and Jane Austen have many books that would qualify for this.

In order to involve my students, I would also take nominations from them for books for the club. I would have this sheet near the bulletin board:

Name _____

Book Recommendation   _____

_____

Why you are recommending this book?

_____

_____

_____

_____

Logic puzzles: Even though I was a social studies teacher, I knew the importance of teaching students logical thinking. Being able to figure something out that you may not know using logic really develops your critical thinking and reasoning skills. One way I did that through my bulletin board enrichment was having logic puzzles for students to work through.

♦ Sudoku: Sudoku is a logic puzzle that develops mathematical thinking. Students are provided with a grid where some of the numbers are filled in, but some are not. Depending on how many boxes there are in the grid box, you are only allowed to use that range of numbers once. In other words, if there are four boxes in the grid, you must use the numbers 1, 2, 3, and 4 with none repeated. In addition, you cannot have the same number across the entire row or column of boxes. It is up to the sudoku solver to determine what numbers go into the missing squares using logic. A sudoku grid might look like this:

3	4	1	
	2		
		2	
	1	4	3

If we are trying to figure out where the 3 goes in the upper, right side grid, we can use clues in the other grids. Since the 3 is in the top row in the upper, left box, we know that the 3 cannot go in that row. And since the 3 is in the furthest right column in the lower, right grid, the 3 cannot go there. That means logically, the only place the 3 can go is in the lower, left hand box of that grid.

I especially like sudoku puzzles because there is a lot of differentiation that can be done with them. You can have a 4 × 4 grid, 6 × 6, the most common 9 × 9, and even 16 × 16. Even within these grids, you can have easy, medium, hard, and expert level puzzles. This allows beginners to those quite skilled at it to participate in this enrichment.

♦ Cryptograms: These are encrypted text where the actual letters used in the statement are substituted with numbers, other letters, or symbols. It is the puzzle solver's task to figure out what this code stands for. Here is an example of a simple cryptogram:

| 1 | 5 | 17 | 9 | 5 | 13 | 4 | 5 | 1 | 1 | 5 | 17 | 9 | 1 | 22 | 10 | 1 | 3 | 14 |

| 1 | 8 | 22 | 20 | 11 | 9 | 18 | 1 | 3 | 5 | 4 |

Using logic, if students can look for patterns or groups, they can deduce what the actual letter is. One you figure out what one of them is, all of the other numbers that are the same become that letter too. One pattern students might notice here is the repetition of two letter words, 1–5, and 17–9. They know one of those two letters has to be a vowel. They may have to use a little trial and error, but let's say they determine the number 5 is the letter O. Then all the 5s become Os. Then since the other letter in the two letter word has to be a consonant, students have a choice of so, do, go, no, or to they can play with. You just continue to use this logic until you get a few numbers figured out, then the rest comes really quickly.

Again, these can be as difficult as you want it to be. You could provide some of the letters for students, you could have simple phrases or long ones, you can have some with less numbers to figure out. You could have a stack of easy, medium, and hard cryptograms at your bulletin board.

♦ Logic grid puzzles: As its name states, this is clues and grids to logically determine what the answers are in a matrix. It looks like this:

Find out who plays what instrument

	Drums	Keyboard	Lead Guitar	Bass Guitar
John				
Paul				
George				
Richard				

1. John cannot play the drums.
2. George and Paul's instruments have strings.
3. George plays the melody.

You read through the clues. A lot of times logic puzzles involve eliminating what it cannot be, and then what is finally left is what can. For example, since John cannot play the drums, you can cross that instrument out. The second clue is that George and Paul's instruments come with strings. That means John's cannot, leaving the only possible instrument he can play to be the keyboard. You can then eliminate John from all other choices. This then indicates that Richard plays the drum since he cannot be the keyboard nor the two guitars. The final clue lets you know George plays the lead guitar because that is the one that plays the melody, leaving Paul to be the bass guitar.

Just as with the others, logic puzzles can be made more challenging either through the number of clues provided, to the number of boxes in the grid. The examples given before is a 1 × 4. You can have a 3 × 4 all the way to 4 × 7. You can also have easy, moderate, and challenging levels.

Current events: A final enrichment bulletin board I had was one involving current events. Being a social studies teacher, I felt it was important that students not only be aware of the history that has happened in the past, but to understand that it still goes on every day. It is also important to know how things taking place on the other side of the planet can affect them, expanding their global awareness.

Over the years, I set up my current events bulletin board a couple of different ways. One way was simply to clip or print up important news stories I would come across, and thumbtack them to the bulletin board. That way when students were walking around the room, they could stop at the current events board and get familiar with this news. Sometimes there were essential questions attached to the article to give students guidance of what they might consider. Other times I would connect where in the world the event took place on a map of the world to teach a little geography as well.

With the advent of the internet and students having instant access to information, I sought to make my current events bulletin board more inter-active. Rather than giving them the news, I offered a scavenger hunt for students to research and learn about events on their own. Every week I would pin up a list of ten terms associated with current events that had been in the news of late. It would look something like this:

- AAPI
- Myanmar
- Suez Canal
- Curiosity
- 2I/Borisov
- Darnella Frazier
- Mozambique
- WHO
- Samia Suluhu Hassan
- Archbishop of Canterbury

Students would have the week to cull the internet and find out what these people, places, organizations, and things had to do with current events. It was stressed to them that they had to indicate the relation of the term to something going on in the world recently. For example, they might be able to identify the Suez Canal as a sea-level waterway located in Egypt, but why is it news? They are going to have to dig a little deeper and discover why this is significant at this time (in this particular case, there was a large ship that ran aground, which caused a huge logjam of ships passing through). Or students might be able to define curiosity as being interested in something, but Curiosity is the name of a rover that was launched to Mars and is being used to explore its surface.

Where Do You Find Resources for Implementing This Strategy?

Depending on how you decide to implement your bulletin boards, most of the materials can be found for free on the internet, including the logic puzzles and brain teasers. The useless trivia and current events might involve some research by the teacher, but this just involves organizing them. The book club might involve the purchase of some books or you could partner with your school librarian to have a shelf in the media center dedicated to your book list. If you want to have the manipulative puzzles available, purchasing a few of these might be necessary, but once you have them they will last for years.

I have posted a few brain teaser, sudoku, riddles, Rebus puzzles, and logic grid puzzles to get you started and to show you what they might look like. They can be accessed at https://www.thegiftedguy.com/resources under the heading of Enrichment Activities.

In addition, I have created some videos called Enrichment With the Gifted Guy that you or students can use to learn how to do some of these activities. Here is a list of them:

- ◆ How to do sudoku https://youtu.be/zIDw7NH2yew
- ◆ How to solve Rebus puzzles https://youtu.be/MmPCPE3Wy7w
- ◆ How to solve logic grid puzzles https://youtu.be/8-kDvPPLXJ0
- ◆ How to solve a cryptogram https://youtu.be/xRV9c8lkw_8

What Impact It Will Have on Your Teaching/ Classroom

This scores a 1 on the impact on teaching scale because these activities may have nothing to do with your curriculum and you do not need to pay them any mind during class other than making sure to switch out the activities from time to time. Your day-to-day lessons and teaching go on as regular with this merely being part of the classroom background that students can choose to engage with or to completely ignore.

The point of enrichment such as this is not to grow the learner necessarily, it is to get them exercising the brain. Just like muscles, in order for the brain to develop, it has to be stretched to its limits. That means accessing the higher levels of Bloom's taxonomy, which brain teasers, logic puzzles, and other such activities do.

In addition, teaching students how to do some of these activities will be a skill they will be able to use the rest of their lives. To this day I do sudoku and logic grid puzzles on my iPad and phone to keep myself sharp. There are also ample opportunities for students to use these activities as a spark to drive their curiosity further. A student might read the first book in a series such as The Ranger's Apprentice and then be intrigued enough to read the other books in the collection. Or if a student were to research one of the current event terms and further explore the history behind it in order to understand its context.

The idea of this kind of enrichment is not that students are required to participate in it and it should definitely not be taken for a grade, but rather they are given opportunities to use their powers of innate curiosity in order to be productive rather than for more diabolical reasons that get them into trouble.

How Much Work It Will Require of You to Successfully Execute It

This enrichment strategy just requires a lot of maintenance, changing the bulletin boards either weekly, monthly, or whenever you deem it needs to be done. Depending whether you decide to provide prizes for students participating in the activities, you might also have to maintain a prize pool that they can choose from. I always had a large, assorted bag of different types of chips or a box with a variety of candy bars in it. You can have healthier fare as well or alternatives to food such as bookmarks, notebooks, and other school supplies.

Board Games That Enrich

Todd Talk Explaining the Strategy
https://youtu.be/ZQlES9Phwl8 [1]

Overview of the Strategy

The premise of this strategy is fairly simple; gather a collection of board games that challenge students cognitively and have them available for use in your classroom. The not so simple part is finding games that do this successfully. For those purposes, I have created a list of games that I feel fit this bill. This is by no means a comprehensive list, but almost all of these games are ones that I have personally played and find them to be good at getting people thinking.

What It Looks Like in the Classroom

These games are available for students to use whenever there is downtime. Downtime could be if class finishes early and there are ten minutes to spare, you host a study hall, indoor recess, the day before a holiday break, and others. Students can go over to the game shelf on their own volition. You are not organizing anything, they choose who they want to play with and what games they want to play. It is an old-fashioned game closet with the new wrinkle of purposefully choosing games that are going to challenge the thinking of students.

Where to Find Resources

There are several games that you could use that fit the description of challenging students. To help you, I have broken them down by subject area or type of thinking.

DOI: 10.4324/9781003238577-2

Math

Sequence: The way this game works, you play a card from your hand, and place a chip on a corresponding space on the game board. Your goal is to get a sequence of five in a row. Each player or team tries to score the required number of five-card SEQUENCES before their opponents. This is a game for 2–12 players so a lot of students could play together. Because students are getting practicing matching, they are developing spatial awareness as sequences can be vertical, horizontal, and diagonal.

Monopoly: The classic game that teaches capitalism, but more important, there is a lot of math involved. Math in paying the bank and receiving change, figuring out how much you owe depending on how many hotels a person has on a space, determine the luxury tax percentage. Up to eight students can play.

Battleship: This is a game where you must guess where your opponent is hiding his or her ships by calling out coordinates. If you call out a coordinate that intersects with any part of the boat, that boat takes a hit. This teaches the mathematical concept of coordinate grids. This is a game for two players.

Yahtzee: This game requires you to roll five dice and to try and create patterns with the rolls. Patterns such as three of a kind, a full house, a straight, or a Yahtzee. It is looking for these patterns and determining the probability of rolling that is using mathematical thinking. You can play with multiple players.

Tenzi: This is a newer game but it is a lot of fun. Each players is given ten dice, all colored the same. A Tenzi means that you roll 10 of the same number. It is a speed game where you keep rolling and rerolling your dice until all ten are the same number, yelling out Tenzi when you complete it. There are variations where you might have to roll two dice at a time and as soon as you get a pair, you have to get another pair, until you have five sets of pairs. Or sixes where you roll your ten dice at the same time as the others playing. If you roll any sixes, they get put into the center, and you gather your remaining dice. You roll those in the next round, again taking out any sixes. First person to roll all sixes wins. Or my personal favorite, Farmzi, where after each roll you must make the sound of a farm animal. It teaches quick number recognition, patterns, and probability. There are some sets of Tenzi with six different colored sets of dice for that many players.

ELA

Boggle: You have a covered box with 16 dice in it with various letters on them. You shake the box and then set it down. Players then look for any words that can be formed by connecting letters that are next to one another while time runs down. When the time is up, you score your words. The longer the word, the more points. There are more advanced versions of the game such as Boggle Deluxe, which has 20 lettered dice and Super Big Boggle, which has 36. As many players can play as can fit around

(*Continued*)

the Boggle box and see the letters. Below is how you score points depending on the length of the word you find:

Word Length
Points
3, 4
1
5
2
6
3
7
5
8+
11

Scrabble: This is a great game for building vocabulary and spelling. Each players draws seven random letters from a bag. When it is their turn, players try and make a word from the letters they have, also using one of the letters on the board. The longer the word, usually the higher the score, although there are bonus boxes spread throughout the board as well as certain non-common letters such as Q and X being worth more. Students can check each other for spelling. You add up your score after laying your tiles, with the game stopping when someone runs out of letters. The person with the highest score is the winner. Can play up to four players.

Rory's Story Cubes: This is more of a fun party game than a someone has to win game. There are nine dice with six unique pictures on each. A person roles however many dice is determined. From the pictures that are rolled, that person must create a story incorporating them. This develops student storytelling ability and creativity. Up to 12 people can play this game.

Scattergories: This is a vocabulary game. There is a die with 20 sides, each with a different letter on it. You roll the dice and then go through three rounds of a list the group has selected. You must come up with words that fit the descriptions on the list that start with the letter you rolled. To add more challenge, if anyone puts the same word as you, you don't get to count it, so originality is important. After the three rounds, people add up how many words they got and the highest wins. This is for up to six players but the reality is you could play with the entire class. The list just needs to be available to all.

(Continued)

Rummy Roots: This is a card game that teaches 42 of the many Greek and Latin roots that make up the English language. There are four games that can be played, increasing in challenge depending on which one you play. Level 1 involves combining two roots to create a word (ex: Auto + Graph = Autograph). Level 3 requires three root words to create a word (ex. Auto + Bio + Graph = Autobiography). It is for up to four players and improves reading comprehension, spelling, dictionary skills, and more.

Social Studies

Risk: The goal of this game is simple: players aim to conquer their enemies' territories by building an army, moving their troops in, and engaging in battle. The strategy however is not so simple. Depending on the roll of the dice, a player will either defeat the enemy or be defeated. Teaches world geography as the board is a map of the world as well as the benefits to alliances and diplomacy. It can have up to six players.

Life: Ah, the game of life. I learned a lot about the adult world playing this game in which you must pursue a career, get married, start a family, buy a house, and make economic decisions throughout the path of life until you are finally able to retire. It teaches economics and how it works in the real world. My favorite aspect is the spaces where life happens such as having to pay for something or something breaks and needs repaired. There is also some math involved with the exchange of money and figuring out how much you owe or need to get paid. You can have up to six players.

Ticket to Ride: This is a good geography game and there are several different versions of the game depending on what geographic area your students need to focus on. There is the United States, Europe, Nordic Countries, France, Japan, Germany, and many others. The goal is to spread your railroads across the land, connecting various sections. The longer the route, the more points you get. Up to five people can play.

Wealth of Nations: This is a fairly complicated game, but once you learn it, there is so much that it teaches. You try and make your nation a world economic superpower by building industries, which allows you to produce commodities. As you build industries, you create ever larger industrial blocs. The larger a bloc is, the greater your return on investment when the bloc produces commodities. The main focus of the game is trade. You must engage in trade to get the commodities that you require. As you build new Industries and earn more money, you acquire Victory Points. The player with the most Victory Points at the end of the game is the winner. You can have as many as six players. You might have to show students how to play at first or have them watch a tutorial on it, but my social studies students really got into it and learned so much about interdependence amongst nations.

Puerto Rico: This is an excellent game for learning how Europe used islands such as Puerto Rico to acquire goods they could not produce themselves. Each player uses a separate small board with spaces for city buildings, plantations, and resources. Shared between the players are three ships, a trading house, and a supply of resources and doubloons. The purpose of the game is to amass victory points by shipping goods to Europe or by constructing buildings. It can be played with up to five players.

Science

Pandemic: This is a great game because it is not about beating each other, but rather working together to try and stop the spread of a deadly virus. The board has several major population centers on Earth. On each turn, a player can use up to four actions to either travel between cities, treat infected populaces, discover a cure, or build a research station. Sprinkled throughout this deck are *Epidemic* cards that speed up and intensify the diseases' activity. Each person plays a different role within the team, and the group must plan together to use their strengths in order to conquer the diseases. There are four roles in the game but players can play in teams.

Evolution: For this game, players adapt their species in an ecosystem where food is scarce and predators lurk. Choosing traits like Hard Shell and Horns will protect your species from Carnivores, while a Long Neck will help them get food that others cannot reach. Although a simple game, the amount of variations make it a new game each time it is played. It can have up to six players.

Operation: The classic game of removing organs and bones from the caricature of a body, while teaching human anatomy. Players are given a set of tweezers and draw cards to see which body part they must remove. If they hit the edge of the opening with the tweezers, a buzzer goes off and you lose your turn. If you are successful, you are awarded money. Up to six people can play this game.

Compounded: The purpose of this game is to build chemical compounds through the management of elements, social play, and trading. Players take on the roles of lab managers, competing to complete the most compounds before they are done so by others – or destroyed in an explosion. Some compounds are flammable and will grow more and more volatile over time; if you take too long to gather the necessary elements for those compounds. Boom. This game can have up to five players at a time.

Totally Gross: Up to four players travel around the game board answering gross questions about science. Land on a Gross-Out space, and you may have to check another player for toe jam or describe the last time you threw up. Every time they answer a question or complete a Gross-Out, players stretch their slime on the scoreline. Stretch it to ten and complete a Lab Experiment to win the game.

Logic

Blokus: One of my personal favorites. For this game with up to four players, you must place various sized pieces onto a playing board, each player taking their turn. The goal is to lay all of your pieces eventually, but they must all be connected by the corners only. Your opponents are trying to stop you from doing this and will block off a strand you are creating. A very good strategy game that is fairly simple to learn and fun. If you want a brief explanation, I have created this Enrichment with the Gifted Guy https://youtu.be/QPBaWLDbcyM.

(Continued)

Clue: The classic whodunit game where players must use deductive reasoning to eliminate suspects, weapons, and rooms before making their guess on who they believe committed the murder. Up to six players take on the roles such as Mr. Green, Mrs. Peacock, and Colonel Mustard.

Set: A card game where each card contains 1–3 objects, with all of the objects on a card having the same color, shape, and shading. Players try to claim sets of cards in a single pass through the deck. A set consists of three cards that are either all alike or all different in each attribute. To start, one person takes the deck and lays out 12 cards face up. The first person to spot a set collects those three cards. After someone has claimed a set, the cardholder lays out three more cards. Whoever gets the most sets wins in this game in which up to 20 can play at one time.

Mastermind: The logic game of learning from your guesses as the code breaker tries and figure out the color pattern of pegs the code maker has arranged. For every guess, the code breaker is given clues in the form of pegs placed by the maker. Your goal is to correctly guess the pattern of the hidden pegs in the least amount of tries. This game is for two players.

Chess: Some would argue this is not a board game but for the purposes of this chapter, it is. Once students learn how all of the pieces move, thousands of strategies can be employed in the quest of capturing your opponent's king. You can get cheap plastic pieces for your game cupboard or splurge a little and get the weighted pieces that last a little longer. Only for two players although you could have several chess sets. If you want a basic tutorial on it, check out this Enrichment with the Gifted Guy https://youtu.be/VkF-9rUoJlo.

Problem Solving

Qwirkle: In this game, you draw wooden blocks with symbols of various colors on them. You then place them either matching colors or shapes, but your line cannot repeat itself, meaning if you are laying blue-colored shapes, none of the shapes can be the same, or if you are laying shapes, none of the colors can be the same. You get points for every block you lay down, building off of what has been laid before or starting a new line from blocks already on the board. If you get six in a line, you are awarded a Qwirkle which is worth 12 points (the six blocks and six bonus points). When blocks have been played, you draw more from the bag so that you have a total of six blocks in your hand. Once all of the blocks have been played, you add up the totals and highest score wins in this four player game.

Hedbanz: Really fun game for up to six players where you have an object attached to your head on a band that everyone else can see but you. You can ask clarifying questions to try to gather clues as to what your object might be. Students much use problem solving to add up all of the clues and guess what is on their head.

Rubik's Race: This is a slide puzzle game where two players face off against one another. You shake the Scrambler and then must make your board match the pattern.

(Continued)

The first person done slams the frame down on their board and it is checked to see whether that person has the correct pattern and has won.

Kanoodle: For two players, a challenge card is played between the players, showing the setup. Each player sets up the game on their own board. When the game starts, players use remaining game pieces to fill up the area on their board, trying not to leave any open spaces. First player to do so wins the round. The game ends after a prearranged number of rounds.

Settlers of Catan: This seems complicated but once learned, is fairly easy to play. Most of the work is in the setup where you place large hexagonal tiles (each showing a resource or the desert) in a honeycomb shape and surround them with water tiles, some of which contain ports of exchange. Number disks, which will correspond to die rolls, are placed on each resource tile. Each player is given two settlements and roads, which are placed on intersections and borders of the resource tiles. Players collect a hand of resource cards based on which hex tiles their last-placed house is adjacent to. A robber pawn is placed on the desert tile. Points are accumulated by building settlements and cities, having the longest road and the largest army, and gathering certain development cards that award victory points. When a player has gathered 10 points, he or she announces the total and claims the win. For up to four players although you can purchase expansion packs to go up to six.

Critical Thinking

Mancala: A fairly simple game but one that will get the brain pumping.

The game is played on a board of two rows, each consisting of six round pits. The rows have a large store at either end called kalah. A player owns the six pits closest to him and the kalah on his right side. Beginners may start with three seeds in each pit, but the game becomes more and more challenging by starting with four, five or up to six seeds in each pit. A player takes all the seeds from one of his pits, and distributes them one by one, counterclockwise, in the pits and the players' own kalah. If the last seed is dropped into an opponent's pit or a non-empty pit of the player, the move ends without anything being captured. If the last seed falls into the player's kalah, you must move again, or capture all contents of the opposite pit. Once all a player's pits are emptied, the game ends and the player who has captured the most pieces is declared the winner.

Spy Alley: For this game for up to six players, each player assumes a secret identity at the start of the game. The object is for each player/spy to collect all the necessary items of their nationality and land on the winner's square. If an opponent guesses your identity before you win though, you are eliminated. If they incorrectly guess, then they are out. Players throw people off the scent by purchasing items of nationalities that they do not need to win.

Codenames: One of my family's favorites. You lay out a grid of cards, 5 × 5, for a total of 25 cards. Each card has a name of something on it. There is the code giver and the code solver. There is a pattern card, which shows which cards belong to which team,

(Continued)

either blue or red. The code giver must provide a single word followed by a number that clues their solver into which cards are theirs and how many of them there are. If the person said games, three, the solver might guess tennis, baseball, and backgammon from the board, and the giver indicates whether these are correct or not. Teams go back and forth until someone has placed all of their team's tiles. For up to eight players.

Azul: This is an abstract strategy board game where players collect sets of similarly colored tiles which they place on their board. When a row is filled, one of the tiles is moved into a square pattern on the right side of the player board where it garners points depending on where it is placed in relation to other tiles on the board. Extra points are scored for specific patterns and completing sets; wasted supplies harm the player's score. The player with the most points at the end of the game wins. Is for up to four players.

7 Wonders: Another game that is seemingly more complicated than it is. You can play with up to seven players, one for each wonder. The name of the game is to gather resources, develop commercial routes and affirm your military supremacy. Build your city and erect an architectural wonder, which will transcend future times. Players do this by drafting cards over multiple rounds, building toward long-term goals, or trying to block your opponents. When the third age is over, players score the points given by their cards and their military conflicts. The winner is the player with the most points.

Creative Thinking

Telestrations: This can be a fairly loud, but fun game that works like the game of telephone, only in this case, you either put a name or draw the object/action on a placard. You pass your placard to the next person who tries to draw or guess your drawing, and it goes around the circle until everyone has had a chance to either draw or guess. The goal is to get your drawing through the entire group with the name of it being the same. You can buy the party edition of this game in which up to ten people can play.

Pictionary: This is like charades only with drawing. You are given a term which you must draw for your partner to guess. You cannot write letters or numbers, only pictures to provide them with clues. If your partner guesses correctly before time runs out, you win a point. There are also all plays where everyone is drawing the same term and the first team to guess correctly gets the point. Can be played with up to 16 players. You just need drawing pads and writing utensils for that many people.

Taboo: Is a group game for up to ten, players take turns describing a word or phrase from a card to their partner without using five common additional words or phrases also on the card. The opposing partners buzz the player describing if one of the five off limits words or phrases is used. The describing team gets a point for each card they guess successfully and the opposing team gets a point for each card they pass on or are penalized on.

(Continued)

Cranium: A great group game for up to 16 players, this requires players to use their whole brain because they must draw, sculpt, act out, or answer trivia questions. For every successful one they answer, they advance in the game until one of the players or teams wins.

Balderdash: For up to six players, cards have real words on them that are not commonly known. The word is read aloud and players must try to come up with definitions that seem like they could be correct. If a majority of the other players guess that your definition is correct, even if it is not, you get the points.

For Younger Kids

Uno: Students will learn numbers and colors in this card game where up to ten students can play. A first card is played and then players either match that color, number, or play a special card. Then the next player must play off of the first player's card, and so on and so forth. First player to get rid of his or her cards is the winner.

Candyland: It teaches colors and basic counting. Players draw a card from the pile and then move along the path to where that next color is. There are various obstacles and penalties to stop you along the way, but the first player to reach the end is the winner. Up to four can play.

Rat-a-tat-Cat: A card game where every player (up to six) is dealt four cards, which they cannot look at. These cards have points values on them. The object of the game is to have the lowest number of points so you draw cards and trade them out for cards in your hand. When you think you have a set of cards lower than your opponents, you can declare Rat-a-tat-Cat. Everyone turns over their cards, they are counted up, and the lowest total wins. It is a good strategy game and teaches basic numbers.

Connect Four: As its name states, you must try and make a pattern of four chips in a row either horizontally, vertically, or diagonally, which your opponent tries to block you. Uses logic and spatial recognition in this game for two.

Sorry: No matter how many times I play this game with my family, I am always impressed with how much strategy is used and how the playing field is fairly even. Players move their colored pieces from start, around the board to home. How you move is determined by the card you draw and if you occupy the space someone has, you send them back to the start. You claim you are sorry, but you are really not.

Notice that nowhere on the list are such games as Trivial Pursuit or Hungry Hungry Hippos. This is because Trivia Pursuit believe it or not does not challenge a person's higher level thinking skills, the answers are all lower-level ones that you would already have to know so no cognitive stimulation is taking place. Hippos on the other hand may work on your hand-eye coordination, but there is not much in the way of thinking taking place. You are more than welcome to have games like this in your classroom, but there are not going to cognitively challenge your students.

You can get these games in a number of ways. You can purchase them yourself. You could ask the PTO or building principal to buy some of the games. You can ask for donations from families. The price of games can add up fairly quickly so build your library slowly, a game here or a game there. After a few years, you will have a pretty comprehensive collection.

What Impact It Will Have on Your Teaching/ Classroom

Little to none. The only way this would affect your classroom is if you decide to use some of these games to teach concepts. For example, my students would play Monopoly when we had our economics unit so that students could see how the spending of money worked. If we were reviewing for a vocabulary or spelling test, we might use something like Scattergories to warm them up. Board games are great teaching tools because they are so fun, students do not even realize they are learning in the process.

How Much Work It Will Require of You to Successfully Execute It

Again, little to nothing. Your role is to gather the games in the first place, make sure there are stored neatly in your game cabinet or whatever (they can tend to get messy after some student use), and make sure students know how to treat the games. You can even have a student whose role is to tidy up the game shelf at the end of the day.

At the beginning of the year, I always had a conversation with students about what the expectations for the board games should be. I allowed them to brainstorm ideas and we would come up with guidelines such as this:

- ◆ Be a good sport
- ◆ Take care of equipment
- ◆ Follow directions of the game
- ◆ Be aware of noise level
- ◆ Be respectful of others

I have found that by setting these guidelines together, students are much more willing to follow them and also to enforce them when they see others violating them. As a result, I have had board games in my class collection last for over a decade.

Makerspace

Todd Talk Explaining the Strategy
https://youtu.be/BjZ8wj5l3VE

Overview of the Strategy

A makerspace means a lot of things to a lot of different people. Some schools have an entire room devoted to their makerspace with all sorts of furniture and equipment such as a 3D printer, band saws and equipment for woodworking, computers, and other expensive items. Not only is such a makerspace cost prohibitive, it would have to be monitored for safety at all times. No, the sort of makerspace I am talking about for the purposes of enrichment is a place students can go to take ideas and bring them to life, to experiment without fear of failure, and to discover using hands-on learning. It is essentially providing a space with some basic supplies and resources to allow kids to take their curiosity and expand upon it.

What It Looks Like in the Classroom

Makerspaces came about during the STEM era and thus a lot of them are devoted to science and engineering, but makerspaces can be created for any classroom. Twenty years ago when I first began teaching gifted and there was no such thing as makerspace, I had what I called "the big box of crap". Essentially I took all of the defunct and broken technology that had accumulated at my house and rather than throwing it away, I put it in a cardboard box and let students rip it apart. Curious students would root through this box, looking at old phones, printers, computers, and VCRs to see what made them tick. There was no guidance on my part, just the opportunity for students to explore and gain an understanding of how things worked.

Makerspaces have come a long way with companies devoted to the sales of mobile carts, Ozobots and other robotics, 3D printers, STEM kits, green screens, LEGO Mindstorms, and various arts and crafts bundles. And if you have the budget to afford such equipment, you are more than welcome to purchase these for your makerspace. However, you can create effective makerspaces without breaking the bank. Here are some ideas for what they might look like in various classrooms:

DOI: 10.4324/9781003238577-3

Science: This is the subject area most connected to makerspaces because of its relationship to STEM. When creating a science makerspace, you want to have supplies that allow students to explore various concepts of science and to experiment. Some things to consider are listed here:

Rocks
Magnets
Batteries
Wire
Balloons
Electrical/Duct tape
Mirror
Food coloring
Aluminum foil
Wax paper
Litmus paper
Funnel
Borax
Bubble wrap
Yeast
Coffee filters
Measuring cups
Baking soda

As you can see, most of these are common household items so you do not need spend a lot of money to get these supplies. If you have the budget you could certainly add some more expensive equipment such as:

Squishy circuits
MakeyMakey Kits
Thermometers
Microscopes
3D Doodler Start
littleBits

Social Studies: Oftentimes we associate social studies as being just history, but there are many other aspects such as geography, culture, government, service learning, and citizenship that can be used to spark a makerspace project. In addition to regular makerspace supplies, you might want to consider for your social studies classroom:

Building materials: This could be Legos, Lincoln Logs, card stock, cardboard, or whatever else students could use to attempt replicas of famous structures in history.

Podcast equipment: This provides students a chance to take something they have learned and try and teach others about it. Usually it would be a microphone and a laptop. Students could also use their phones.

Maps: These could be a wall map, could be placemat maps, could be road maps, even old maps.

Old textbooks: These often can be used to see how history has changed over time.

Flags: These include either a poster or mini versions of flags from around the world. These will hopefully spark interest in them exploring the cultures of these.

Children's books in other languages: Even at the junior high and high school level, students can use the pictures as context clues to learn about their language.

English: For ELA, one consideration for your makerspace is to create a writer's workshop. This can take many forms but the general idea is it is a place students can go to create stories. This may be written stories, videos, audiobooks, and so on. You would want to have equipment that would allow students to jumpstart their imagination and storytelling. Some things to consider are as follows:

Magnetic poetry: These are words and phrases printed on a small magnet that students can manipulate to form sentences and stories. It is good for brainstorming and students can put these on metal boards and leave them for others to see.

Library: One of the best ways tolearn to write is by reading. Having a small library of books that are age-appropriate that they can go into the makerspace and be read to look for inspiration and study the craft of writing.

Sticky notes/index cards: These allow students to break their stories into scenes and to storyboard them. These can also be easily manipulated to change the order of events or add/delete scenes.

Legal pads/notebook paper/clipboards: Having something students can jot ideas on and develop their stories with. Nothing is as magical as a blank piece of paper just waiting to be filled.

Comfortable furniture: Writing can be an exercise in endurance depending on what you are sitting on while doing it. Having comfortable furniture so that students are focusing more on their ideas than their aching behind can help the writing process. This might even be having rugs students can lay on and unwind.

Pencils and colored pens: Nothing is more important to the writing process if writing by freehand than a good writing utensil that just allows the ideas to flow from your hand to the paper.

Laptops with video: Students can type their stories onto an electronic document, or film scenes using the laptop's camera. There are plenty of programs that allow students to create their own stories as well as edit video.

Posters with writing tips: To be used as inspiration, these posters act as reminders to writers about their craft and what they should think about. Some examples of posters would be this one showing story structure:

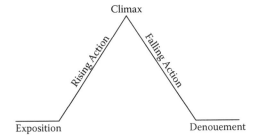

Math: This is a subject not always considered to be hands-on, but the more you can have students using math in this manner, the more relevant they are going to find it. It can also turn the abstract idea of math into a more concrete form.

Jars of things to count
Math manipulatives
Dominoes
Paper for origami
Measurement tools
Math flash cards
Whiteboards
Play paper money
Advertisers
Wooden cubes

General: This would not be subject specific but would just be a place where students can challenge themselves and think outside the box. Because it is general there doesn't need to be a whole lot of structure although there can be. Simply providing the space and materials might be good enough. Here is a list of general supplies you might want to consider for your makerspace:

Copy Paper	Cardboard	Index Cards
Construction paper	Tape	Rubber bands
Glue/glue sticks	Paper/plastic cups	Tissue Paper
Fabric	Play-Doh	Cotton balls
Chenille sticks	Beads	Paper plates/bowls
Plastic silverware	Binder/paper clips	Yarn
Tin foil	Popsicle sticks	Toothpicks
Straws	Ping pong balls	Toilet paper rolls

What the set-up for your makerspace might look like is how it best fits into your classroom. It could be in the corner, it could be in a common space in the hallway, it could be along the entire back wall. You might have an alcove in your room where you could house it. It does not however require a ton of space. Simply a table with some chairs or seating and a shelf or cabinet where materials can be stored. This is what the makerspace looks like at one of the elementary buildings in my district.

Materials are stored in bins on a shelf along the back wall and there are tables the students can bring the bins back to in order to start on their projects. Does not take up much space at all and yet still gives students plenty of choices.

Where to Find Resources

Once you have established what you want your makerspace to look like, you need to figure out what supplies you are going to need and how to get these. You don't have to purchase all of these materials. There are practical ways you can supply your makerspace:

- Student supply list
- Parent/Business donations
- Supply closet
- Garage sales/thrift stores
- Recycling bins
- Storage rooms
- Retiring/moving teachers
- PTO
- Gifted coordinator

There are also some books that I keep on my shelf that have wonderful project or task ideas that you can use with students. These books are listed here:

- *The Elementary School Library Makerspace* – Marge Cox
- *The Big Book of Makerspace Projects* – Colleen Graves and Aaron Graves
- *Makerspaces in School* – Lacy Brejcha

What Impact It Will Have on Your Teaching/ Classroom

Most of the work comes in the setting up of the makerspace such as amassing supplies and providing guidance to those working in the space. If structured clearly, it will not require much of your attention during the actual class. Students will just gravitate toward the space if they are finished with their work and create whatever they choose. If the makerspace is off in the corner, other students may not even notice a student or two has gone over and begun to work on something.

How Much Work It Will Require of You to Successfully Execute It

You can decide how you want your makerspace to work. Here is a spectrum of different structures:

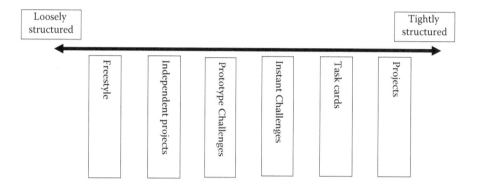

Freestyle: This is just about making the materials and space available to the students but letting them create whatever they want. There is no end goal in mind, it is just to provide a place where students can be creative and to explore their own ideas. This might look like a student sitting down and constructing a chenille stick flower because it is what pops into her head.

Independent projects: These are a bit more structured in that students do have an end product in mind. There is a purpose to their creating, but they still get complete control for what this is and for what purpose. What this might look like is a student likes a certain videogame character and decides to create a model of this character using the materials in the makerspace.

Prototype challenges: Here students are given a very basic premise and then they decide where they are going to take it. These might be listed on index cards or put on sticky notes and adhered to the wall. An example would be one where it asks a student to create a better version of a phone.

Instant challenges: These present a challenge and tell students what materials they can use and what purpose their product would have, but still lets students decide how these materials will be used and in what fashion. It might be a challenge that students create a bridge using only toothpicks, clay, and paper clips that stretches across a one foot gap.

Task cards: These are cards with a bit more guidance than just the prototype challenge. It might say create a container that can carry your lunch and has a handle. Students would then set out to build this but the purpose is established by the task card.

Projects: This is a long-term project that asks students to create a product that solves a clear purpose. Materials might even be determined for the student. One such project might be making an insect bot where students are given the materials they can use and demonstrates the body parts based off of a real insect.

Whichever one of these structures you decide to use will determine how much work you will have to do. Instant challenges, task cards, and projects don't write themselves. These would either have to be create or procured by the teacher and then displayed at the makerspace. The freestyle and independent project requires very little work by the teacher, but its lack of structure can make for mixed results where the student might not be able to produce anything without some sort of guidance.

No matter which structure you choose, one thing that will always be required is organizing and resupplying the makerspace. Things can get messy real fast, so making sure to establish norms or expectations for those working in the makerspace can help, but you will still have to do some tidying up at the end of the class or day. You can always assign students to do this as well.

Four Corners

Todd Talk Explaining the Strategy
https://youtu.be/wSbgTOvW0RY [1]

Overview of the Strategy

The way school is set up as an institution is quite inorganic. There is an allotted time per class and teachers feel obligated to fit enough work in that time to keep the student occupied (and hopefully learning). We know though that students learn at different paces. You might have allotted 30 min to work on an activity. Some students need only 15 min, while others are only halfway done at the end of class. Yet as teachers we feel compelled to try and keep everyone at the same place, asking our accelerated students to slow down and the ones falling behind to catch up. What if instead of trying to slow these students down, we allow them to finish early and then give them opportunities to satiate their curiosity by exposing them to high interest projects that will allow them to be enriched.

What It Looks Like in the Classroom

In my social studies classroom I had a desk or table set up in each of the four corners of the room. At a couple of these, I had computers, others had books, while others had additional resources that might be needed. At each of these was a project with a description, a suggested product, and a starting point. I explained to students at the beginning of the school year how the four corners worked. If a student got done with an assignment early, he was more than welcome to go to one of the corners that piqued his interest and to explore the project there. I told students they did not have to work on the project every day, but whenever they had downtime in class, which could be before class started, if they had finished their assessment while others were still working on it, or at the end of the class. It might take a student multiple weeks to complete the project, and there were some students who stopped working on the project because they become disinterested or just didn't have time. But there were many who found it interesting enough to complete.

DOI: 10.4324/9781003238577-4

Here was some examples of projects I had in my corners:

The X-Files Corner

Objective

To research a historical mystery and analyze various theories to determine which one is the most plausible.

Materials

- ◆ Choose one of the following:
  - Big Foot
  - Loch Ness Monster
  - Lost Colony of Roanoke
  - Easter Island
  - Stonehenge
  - Disappearance of Amelia Earhart
  - Assassination of John F. Kennedy
  - Bermuda Triangle
  - Atlantis
  - Lizzie Borden
  - O.J. Simpson murder case
  - Construction of Pyramids
  - Lindbergh Baby Kidnapping
  - Jack the Ripper
  - Jon Benet Ramsey Murder
  - Salem Witch Trials
  - Can come up with your own X-File

Lesson

The student will be looking at unsolved occurrences and comparing different possible theories, determining which one seems the most likely. They will use eyewitness accounts, scientific data, and other sources they find on the subject. They must weigh the following:

- ◆ Bias
- ◆ Different points of view
- ◆ Reliable versus unreliable sources
- ◆ Multiple sources
- ◆ Hard scientific data (if any)

(Continued)

Product

The culmination of this research will result in a detailed paper. The student will use at least two different sources covering the phenomenon to write their paper. The paper investigates three possible theories on the subject and determines which one if any is the most possible one. Must use examples to back decision up. Could also create a slide presentation as an alternative.

Ranking Ohio's Presidents Corner

Objective

Ohio has had eight presidents" William Henry Harrison, Ulysses S. Grant, Rutherford B. Hayes, James Garfield, Benjamin Harrison, William McKinley, William Taft, and Warren Harding. The question though is: Which one was the best (or the worst)?

Materials

Website http://touringohio.com/trivia/ohio-presidents.html will give you a little background information on the presidents.

Lesson

Which of these men was the best at being the president and what is the basis for the argument. You will have to weigh the following:

- ◆ What accomplishments they had as president?
- ◆ Was there anything they did wrong while in office?
- ◆ Could they have done a better job?
- ◆ Were they popular with the American people?
- ◆ What is their legacy?

Product

You will rank the presidents from 1 to 8, giving reasons for your decision and comparing and contrasting their time in the White House. You will display this on a poster, tri-fold, slide show, WeVideo, or some other product of your choice.

What If corner?

Objective

Students will take a look at an important historical event and suppose what might have changed if things had gone differently? Would the world be altered and how so?

(Continued)

Materials

- ◆ Books with which to generate ideas.
  - • Almost America
  - • What If?
- ◆ History books with which to model the entry in the history book after.

Lesson

Things could be very different if a certain historical event had gone a different way. For instance, what if the British had won the American Revolution, or if the Romans had never adapted Christianity as their official religion, or maybe things would be much different if the Native Americans had developed more advanced weapons than the Europeans. Students must select an important historical event and imagine if things had gone differently. Then students must predict how this alternate version would change the history books. They must look at:

- ◆ What would be different?
- ◆ How would this change history?
- ◆ Would this change be minor or massive?
- ◆ What about this change shows the importance of this historical event?

Product

Students will then rewrite the history books. They will make an entry for a history book or Wikipedia article with their changes, giving an overview of the event and its significance in history. This entry can include photos, charts and graphs, maps, and other tools. Students will be evaluated on their creativity as well as the use of information to back the predictions they have made.

History in Literature Corner

Objective

Students will read either a historical fiction, biography, or interpretation of an event or people. From this reading, students will judge the author's point of view and see whether there is any bias contained within.

Materials

- ◆ Various books contained on the two shelves in the cabinet.
- ◆ Students can select books other than these but they must be approved.

Lesson

Students will choose one of the books and read it. As they read it, they will be looking for the following:

(Continued)

- ♦ An overall understanding of the book and the topic it covers.
- ♦ The main theory of the book. What is the book trying to do? Is it portraying its subject as a hero or a flawed character? Is it criticizing the event that took place or praising it? What is the author's main intent by writing this book?
- ♦ Is the author biased in his or her presentation or simply giving a straight-forward report on the subject? If he or she is biased, how so?
- ♦ Did the student like the book? What did they learn from it? Could the book have been better and how?

Product

After finishing the book, the student will create a dusk jacket for the book using a piece of paper about the size of a textbook cover. The dust jacket should not be a copy of the one already on the book, but rather an original creation of the student. The dust jacket will contain three parts to it.

- ♦ A cover with an illustration that conveys the author's main theory of the book. They say a picture is worth a thousand words and this picture should show what the book is about. It can be a photograph, an illustration from an artist, or a drawing of your own. Below the picture should be a brief description of what this picture tells us about the book.
- ♦ An inside front and back flap synopsis of the book. What is the book about? Sort of like a book report without any opinion. Simply a straightforward summary of the book.
- ♦ Back cover will be a book review written by the student. This is where the student will give their opinion of the book. Did they like it or not? Why or why not? What could have been done to improve the book? What the author biased in their reporting of the event or person?

I did not count these four corners projects as part of their grade, but did provide feedback on what they had produced. I rotated in new projects every nine weeks so that if a student didn't find something interesting the first time, they might the next round. Although it was not tied to any specific content standards, I focused on specific skills.

Where to Find Resources

You can take any project and turn it into a four corners project. The thing you need to be sure of is that these are projects that can be done independently.

Here are some projects that could be used as four corners projects, one from each core subject area:

ELA

What If Cinderella Had Gold Slippers Instead of Glass Ones?

Brief Description
Folktales have been around for hundreds of years but different cultures have different variations on the same story. For instance, in the Disney version of Cinderella, she has a magical fairy godmother. In the Iraq version, the godmother is in the form of a red fish while in the Egyptian version it is a god. What do these stories indicate about the culture they come from? You will read an American folktale and compare it to the version from a foreign country, analyzing what the events, characters, and moral indicate about the country it was written in.

Product
You will write an analysis comparing the US version to the foreign one, saying what the differences say about the cultures. You might even want to rewrite the folktale to give it a perspective.

Skills
Identify the influence of setting on the selection.
    Describe the cultural practices and products of various groups.

Starting Point
Read the two versions of Cinderella from different cultures.

Suggested Materials
Books with folktale from a foreign country.
Book on culture about that country.

Math

You Are What You Eat

Brief Description
Counting calories has become a general practice among those trying to live healthier lives. It also is a chance to use some math skills, adding the calories together and subtracting them from your allotment for the day.

(Continued)

Product

You will count your calorie intake for your meals for a period of three weeks, keeping a log of what you eat followed by the amount of calories. At the end of the three weeks, you will write an analysis of your food habits, what you eat that is low or high in calories and other patterns that you notice. You will need to display your calorie intake on a chart, graph, or other graphic organizer.

Skills

Compare different representations of the same data and evaluate how well each representation shows important aspects of the data, and identify appropriate ways to display the data.

Starting Point

Read the chart of breakfast foods and figure out what you could eat if you were limiting your calorie intake to 400 calories.

Suggested Materials

Journal to log your calorie intake
Food
Calculator

Science

A Hero Just Ain't a Type of Sandwich

Brief Description

Spider-Man was created when a radioactive spider bit him on the hand. The Fantastic Four got their amazing powers when they were exposed to a cosmic storm in space. The Hulk was exposed to gamma rays, which turned him into a monster every time he got angry. Science has created many of the superheroes we have come to enjoy.

Product

You will create a new superhero, drawing a comic book chronicling the adventures of this superhero who got his/her power from a scientific accident. The origin must explain what scientific principles caused the powers and how they work. The powers must be one of the following:

- ◆ Controlling the wind
- ◆ Controlling the weather
- ◆ Create ice
- ◆ Cause physical changes
- ◆ Cause chemical changes

(Continued)

- ◆ Change into different states (i.e. solid, liquid, gas)
- ◆ Raise or lower temperature

Skills
Whichever power is chosen must be explained using the standard.
Use organizational strategies to plan writing.

Starting Point
Read Spider-Man comic

Suggested Materials
Drawing paper
Pencils/pens/markers

Social Studies

Seven Wonders of the World

Brief Description
Out of the seven wonders of the ancient world, only the Pyramids of Giza still exist today. What made these structures a wonder and what purpose did they serve?

Product
You will research the ancient seven wonders of the world and why they are a wonder. Then you will create a list of what you believe to be the seven modern wonders of the world, explaining why you chose the structures that you did and determining will they last for centuries as the pyramids have. You may create models of these structures to aid in your explanation.

Skills
Formulate a question to focus research.
List questions and search for answers within the text to construct meaning.

Starting Point
Watch YouTube video on The Seven Wonders of the World https://www.youtube.com/watch?v=86FyWTKzxpI

Suggested Materials
Internet research on the seven wonders of the world.
Internet research on architectural wonder of the modern world.

You can be as specific or as general with these projects as you like. The advantages to being specific is that students know exactly what to do, but the disadvantage is that it requires a lot of planning for you and does not give students much choice. If you are general, students may not know exactly what to do and will need clarification, meaning they are not working as independently as you would hope. This does, however, provide students with a lot of autonomy, which will make them even more interested in working on the project. You could have a project such as this:

You Create the Project

Brief Description
Taking one of the content area standards, you create a project about something you would like to learn.

Product
Your choice, but must show mastery of the skill that you have set as your learning objective.

Skills
Must choose learning objective(s) to focus the project on.

Starting Point
You find one.

Suggested Materials
Once again, your choice.

You will find some four corner project ideas for all four core subject areas available on my website www.thegiftedguy.com/resources. You may also want to use one of my many books with project examples in them that could be adapted to a four corners project. These can be found at https://www.amazon.com/Todd-Stanley/e/B0052XUQ2W/ref=dp_byline_cont_pop_book_1. You could create your own four corners projects that are specific to your classroom that you think might help build skills students will need.

What Impact It Will Have on Your Teaching/ Classroom

There should be little impact on your teaching or classroom if you provide enough structure and guidance so that a student will be able to do the work independently without bombarding you with a ton of questions. Although you can field the occasional question, you will still be working with the rest of the class during this time.

How Much Work It Will Require of You to Successfully Execute It

Most of the work on the teacher's end would be providing the projects. How much work this requires is dependent on whether you use already-existing projects, or you decide to create your own. No matter which method you choose you have to make sure there are the proper resources that will enable students to work by themselves. That means if students need to read a book as a starting point, that you have a copy in that corner. Or if there are specific supplies students might need to create their product, you have those readily available in the corner so that the student is disrupting class as little as possible. If you are pointing students toward certain websites, you would want to either provide a computer and bookmark these sites, or if students are to use their own computers, giving them the links to those sites.

It also means refreshing the projects every once in a while so that students have choices. I rotated my projects every nine weeks, meaning I had to have 16 projects for the year. If you have the same four projects all year long, you will probably find the corners gathering dust by the end of the year.

Enrichment Clubs

Todd Talk Explaining the Strategy
https://youtu.be/pnRIBBA0VxE. [1–3]

Overview of the Strategy

Enrichment clubs are clubs that you offer to students that are most times not directly tied to your curriculum. They are typically interest-based clubs, but ones that are designed to challenge students and their thinking. An example of a club that I have run for many years is chess club. Chess does not teach anything specifically related to any curriculum taught in school, but it teaches some very valuable skills and thinking as follows:

- Improved memory
- Deeper focus
- Increased self-awareness
- Forced to think before you act
- Planning skills
- Prioritization
- Creativity
- Problem-solving skills
- Sportsmanship
- Exercise for both sides of the brain

As a result, I am willing to teach students how to play, knowing it is a lifelong skill with many benefits.

There are two different types of enrichment clubs:
1. National Programs: This involves connecting with an organization that has already developed curriculum and has chapters all over the state and nation. The advantages of course is that you do not have to reinvent the wheel. For many of these programs such as Math Counts and Word Masters, they provide you with the problems and work that students will be doing. Even if they do not supply you with the work, they provide you with a framework and parameters to use with students. Destination Imagination, Battle of the Books, Invention Convention, Model United

DOI: 10.4324/9781003238577-5

Nations, and First Lego Robotics all provide students with a general path to follow. And nearly all of these have an authentic competition aspect where students compete with other schools, showing what they have learned for the year. Your club time would just be students preparing and working toward this.

2. Homegrown Clubs: There are clubs that are based on student interest or a building need. Some of these that I have been involved with over the years are school newspaper, drama club, eco club, STEM, creative writing, student tutoring, and book clubs. Some were formed because I polled students about what they would like to do such as eco club and creative writing. Book clubs have started organically based on a hot book that a lot of the students are reading at the time. Other clubs were formed because my principal wanted his building to have opportunities for students to get involved such as the school newspaper and student tutoring. Some were just ones that I had an interest in offering such as STEM and chess. Many of these we made it up as we went along, using student input to determine the path we took. As the advisor though I felt it was my obligation to have a general idea of what we would be doing for the year with an authentic product at the end. In the creative writing club the end goal was for students to submit a short story to a teen writing contest. Then each club meeting was about learning the writing process including basic story structure, developing ideas, construction of the plot, writing dialogue and action, and revising and editing.

You can also have a hybrid version of these two. I liked what the Future City Competition program allowed my elementary students to do, but students must be in sixth to eighth grades in order to compete. So I took the general idea of Future City, using Sim City to design a city, having to create a model, giving a public presentation, and modified it for my younger audience. Even though we did not compete in the state competition, we made sure to have an authentic showcase of their work.

What It Looks Like in the Classroom

This strategy can be set up quite differently depending on your schedule, resources, and how well it ties to your curriculum. I have run enrichment clubs in the following ways before:

Before/After School: Either an hour right before school or after school, having a dedicated time and space for students to be involved in the club. I would usually have announcements for a couple of weeks and have students sign up (making sure parents were aware they would have to drop off or pick up). I did not strictly limit these clubs to gifted students, but found that when I offered them, these were the students they tended to attract. I asked students to commit to coming every week because many times we were building upon what we were doing. I did not have a fee associated with it because I didn't want cost to preclude anyone from participating. Because it is outside of the regular school day, this obviously takes a commitment by the teacher. I often times offered this time slot because it would allow me to offer it to the entire school rather than just my students. I especially targeted the schools in my district that were title 1 schools with this time slot because I didn't want students to be unable to participate because it was on a weekend or in the evening. I found that before or just after school caused the likelihood of parents being willing to transport their kids to be much higher.

Dedicated time during the week: I was fortunate to be on two teaching teams that saw the value in such enrichment clubs. Every Friday afternoon we put our regular classes aside and each teacher on the team was responsible for running a club. Teachers chose something they were passionate about so it didn't seem like more work, and we let students choose their top three clubs, assigning them to one of these depending on the demand. This was a typical breakdown of the clubs offered:

- Mrs. Ma. – Photography
- Mrs. Or. – Invention Convention
- Mrs. Mu. – Coding
- Mrs. B. – Model United Nations
- Mrs. J. – Art club
- Mrs. L. – Fitness club
- Mrs. Ov. – Battle of the Books
- Mr. S. – Chess club
- Mrs. S. – Robotics
- Mrs. D. – Public speaking club

We held these clubs the last hour of the school day. Some of them were ongoing, year-long clubs, while others may have new activities each meeting such as art, fitness, chess, and photography. The nice thing about these clubs was that we mixed homerooms and grade levels, so students were getting to work and interact with students they didn't normally get the chance to. We ran these clubs for the entire school year and although we were giving up some class time, we knew ultimately that students were learning other valuable skills that the content areas could not provide.

Part of school-wide clubs: I have worked with a couple of schools who ran clubs for the entire school. This allowed more options for offerings. A couple of these schools were "Leader in Me" schools, which used the philosophy of Steven Covey and his seven habits of highly effective children:

- Habit 1: Be Proactive
- Habit 2: Begin With the End in Mind
- Habit 3: Put First Things First
- Habit 4: Think Win-Win

♦ Habit 5: Seek First to Understand, Then to Be Understood
♦ Habit 6: Synergize
♦ Habit 7: Sharpen the Saw

Every club made an effort to promote these habits and to encourage students to use them in their club work.

Here were the clubs that were offered school-wide:

STEM	Puzzle Pack	Sewing/Knitting
Green and Clean	Yoga	Running Club
Book Worms	Craft/Scrapbooking	Movement and Mindfulness
Power of the Pen	Gardening	Jump Rope
Girl Power	Invention Convention	Community Service
Kids Who Cook	Music	Newspaper Team
Chess and Games	Coloring Club	Reading Club
Leave and Legacy	Brain Works	Young Gents

The idea here was that every other week the entire school was going to enrichment clubs. We held town hall meetings showcasing what some of the groups were doing before dismissing the students to their designated club.

I liked this particular set up because it really created a sense of school community. Kids from various grades were mixed together and many of the clubs were about making the school a better place. It also allowed teachers to work with different kids from around the school and form relationships with them.

Weekend warriors: I have had to use this with older students, or when we have students at different schools or busy sports schedules make after-school clubs difficult to hold. Instead we would have a meeting on the weekend. Clubs such as Destination Imagination, Science Olympiad, and Model United Nations would be run on a Saturday. I would open the school and students would conduct a practice to get them prepared for the coming competition. This was not the most ideal situation as I was giving up some of my precious weekend time, but knowing this was the only time students could participate.

Part of your curriculum: The best scenario is when you can offer a club as part of your class because it lines up with your curriculum. I could justify taking three weeks of science class to do Invention Convention with students because it aligned with the 6th grade Next Generation Science Standards:

♦ Define the criteria and constraints of a design problem with sufficient precision to ensure a successful solution.
♦ Evaluate competing design solutions using a systematic process to determine how well they meet the criteria and constraints of the problem.

- ◆ Analyze data from tests to determine similarities and difference among several design solutions to identify the best characteristics of each that can be combined into a new solution.
- ◆ Develop a model to generate data for iterative testing and modification of a proposed object, tool, or process such that an optimal design can be achieved.

Similarly, Model United Nations met several standards for my social studies class dealing with civic participation:

- ◆ Individuals can better understand public issues by gathering and interpreting information from multiple sources. Data can be displayed graphically to effectively and efficiently communicate information.
- ◆ Civic participation requires individuals to make informed and reasoned decisions by accessing and using information effectively.
- ◆ Individuals make the community a better place by solving problems in a way that promotes the common good.

There are some schools that offer elective classes such as Mock Trial or Robotics. Students can then work on these year-long. However you decide to offer it to students will dictate how much interference it will have on your own life.

Where to Find Resources

Almost all of the national programs have active websites that give you a good idea of how to get involved. Some are better than others while some of these programs also have state sites that will let you know what chapter governs the area your school is in. Here are some of the major national programs that I am familiar with and their website:

Competition	Ages/ Grades	Website
Battle of the Books	Grades 3–12	https://www.battleofthebooks.org/
Destination Imagination	Ages K–12	https://www.destinationimagination.org/
First Lego League	Ages 9–16	https://www.firstlegoleague.org/
Future City Competition	Grades 6–8	https://futurecity.org/
Future Problem Solving	Ages 8–18	https://www.fpspi.org/

(Continued)

Competition	Ages/ Grades	Website
Invention Convention	Grades K-8	https://inventionconvention.org/home-page/
Linguistics Olympiad	Grades 6–12	https://ioling.org/
Math Counts	Grades 6–8	https://www.mathcounts.org/
Math League	Grades 3–6	https://www.mathleague.com/
Model United Nations	High school	https://www.nmun.org/
Odyssey of the Mind	Grades K-12	https://www.odysseyofthemind.com/
Physics Bowl	High school	https://www.aapt.org/programs/physicsbowl/
Rube Goldberg Competition	Grades 6–12	https://www.rubegoldberg.com/contests/
Science Olympiad	Grades 6–12	https://www.soinc.org/
Speech and Debate	Grades 9–12	https://www.speechanddebate.org/
Word Masters Challenge	Grades 3–8	https://www.wordmasterschallenge.com/

I have created a few video Todd Talks on programs that I have personally been involved in. They will provide you with an overview and how I used them in my classes.

National Enrichment Clubs https://youtu.be/u6yuUQCq-zk
Invention Convention https://youtu.be/Gcs2m_9wI1w
Model United Nations https://youtu.be/R8gOKU47JlE
Destination Imagination https://youtu.be/rGAKS2P6Ffs

I have also written an entire book on these sorts of enrichment activities available through Prufrock Press titled *Enrichment Activities for Gifted Students: Extracurricular Academic Activities for Gifted Education*. This book explains in great detail a variety of national academic extra-curricular activities that students can get involved with as well as some homegrown ones. It is broken up by subject areas as well as skills developed.

As for homegrown clubs, I tried as much as possible to allow the students to steer the club where it was going to go. For an eco club I ran at one of the middle schools, the group decided that it wanted to build and maintain a compost bin. This involved them raising the money to buy materials, actually building it, and then creating a schedule so that every lunch period had a representative that would ensure leftovers made it into the compost bin as well as keeping up with its maintenance.

What Impact It Will Have on Your Teaching/ Classroom

Notice I had a 1 thru 3 for the impact on teaching. The variable for this ranking is whether you are running it as an extra-curricular club, or is it cocurricular, which means it is part of your class. Programs such as DECA and BPA are run through vocational classes.

If you are doing this as a before, after, or extra-curricular club, then the impact on your teaching will be a 1. However, if it ties in with your curriculum, every student is doing it, and you are evaluating it, it would be a 3. If you have to cut into your Fridays or you do it as part of a during school club, the impact might be a 2 because you are losing limited class time.

How Much Work It Will Require of You to Successfully Execute It

Most of these enrichment clubs require management more than anything. If you are running a chess club you might need to provide students with boards, pieces, and a space to play, but once they get started you can just let them play. You might have the occasional lesson or you might need to show beginners how to move certain pieces, but for the most part, students are playing one another. There are others such as Destination Imagination where it is actually a penalty if you interfere with your team. Students are to generate all of the ideas, find all of the resources, and do all of the work. You just provide them a space, the structure they will be following, and maybe some snacks. Science Olympiad might require you organizing the team and assigning roles, but the students are the ones doing most of the work. I know a teacher who runs the Dungeons and Dragons club for his school and he doesn't even know how to play. He just had students with a desire to play so he allows his classroom to be used after school and is merely there as the responsible adult.

To be involved with some of the national programs can cost money. For a team to get started in First Lego Robotics here is a cost rundown:

Start-up Costs	Costs	Notes
National registration	$225	Varies by county
Local competition registration	$120–$320	Varies by region

(Continued)

Start-up Costs	Costs	Notes
FLL table	$75–$100	
FLL EV3 robot set	$496	Includes expansion
SPIKE prime set through FLL	$410	$8 Shipping; includes expansion
FLL challenge set	$75	Can vary by country; $15 shipping
Laptop/Computer	$0–$1000	Can reuse existing laptop
Supplies	$25	Trifold, markers, glue, binders

There are those that are less expensive. Invention Convention prides itself that there is no cost for students to participate, but there are supplies to build the invention model as well as trifold and art supplies. You can go to the websites of these organizations to get a good idea of how much it costs for students to participate before you decide to become involved.

Even if there is a cost, you may be able to get your district to support such clubs. The district I am in supports the Business Professional of America, Destination Imagination, Model United Nations, Youth and Government, Math Counts, Mock Trial, Continental Math League, Word Masters, and National Geography Bee, just to name a few.

Bonus Opportunities

Todd Talk Explaining the Strategy
https://youtu.be/2bdDqYfYAn4 [2]

Overview of the Strategy

Just as the name implies, a bonus opportunity is the chance for a student to challenge themselves by choosing whether they are going to extend their learning either through additional questions on a homework assignment, the chance to create something that puts what they are learning into play, or whether it is deciding to answer a tougher question on an assessment because they think they have a good understanding of it.

This is different than extra credit. When I first began teaching, I would offer extra credit questions on my assessments such as this:

Worth 2 points
Name the original set of laws created to govern the United States of America?

As you can discern, this is not enrichment. This is seeing whether students were paying attention, remembering something I might have mentioned just once or twice or that they saw in the textbook while reading about the formation of the Constitution. This is not going to stretch the minds of these students nor will it challenge them. After a few years, I stopped giving extra credit and instead began to offer bonus opportunities. These were designed to enrich kids by extending their thinking or pushing them into a greater understanding of what they were learning.

Instead of the extra credit question, I would offer a bonus opportunity question:

If you could have made a law at the formation of the United States, what would it have been and what would be your reasoning for suggesting it?

This is different from the extra credit because that is giving a single correct answer in order to receive credit. Everyone's answer would be the same. This bonus opportunity expands the thinking by asking the opinion of the student, but an opinion that would have to be based on the understanding of the laws that were made, as well as justifying the decision he

DOI: 10.4324/9781003238577-6

made, which is in the higher levels of Bloom's rather than the lower level recall of the extra credit question. Likely no response would be the same.

An example of a bonus opportunity I did in the middle of a lesson was when we were studying the Indian Mounds, looking at all of the things that have been found in them and why they might have been put there. I offered two bonus opportunities for students to go deeper into the learning. Because we were in Ohio where there are over 70 mounds spread throughout the state such as the Serpent Mound and the Hopewell Mounds, I told students they could take a trip to one of these mounds with their family and take pictures of it, also indicating what was found in these mounds. We had mounds as close as 15 minutes away, although I had some families who traveled over two hours to explore a mound.

If a student was not able to travel, I had an additional bonus opportunity. They could create their own Indian Mound either in a model, or my one student who actually built one in his back yard, burying items that he felt represented our society. He brought in pictures and explanations of why he chose the items he did.

Sometimes I counted this into their grade, sometimes I did not, but I made sure students knew which one when I introduced it. Interestingly, I had about the same amount of students decide to do the bonus opportunity whether it was offered as a grade or not.

What It Looks Like In the Classroom

A bonus opportunity can be introduced in many aspects of the classroom. For example, here is a bonus opportunity that could be offered to deepen the homework. If the homework was to read chapters in the book *The Life of Pi*, these questions can be given to students that are not content based but rather questions to consider as they read:

◆ Would the book be told differently if the main character were not from India?
◆ Why do you suppose the author chose a tiger to be in the boat with them?
◆ How would you predict how this story is going to end or what will happen next?
◆ Is the setting of the lifeboat important to the book or could it be just as effective somewhere else?

Students are not required to answer these questions or turn them in for a grade. They are simply guidance to help students to ponder and think about the book. You might use questions similar to this in class discussion, but they are not meant to check for compliance.

You could use a bonus opportunity reflection for students to think about after they have finished the work you have asked them to. If you assign a set of problems for students in a math class, at the end of the assignment you could ask these questions:

- ♦ How would you use this skill in your own life?
- ♦ Is there a simpler way to figure these out?
- ♦ Which question did you think was the most difficult and why?
- ♦ How would you explain how you solved these to a friend?

This gets students thinking about how math shows up in the real world, a connection that is valuable for them to make. Bonus opportunities should not be about offering students more problems or read more chapters. They are meant to enrich.

You could use bonus opportunities in your projects. Here was a project I had for students when we were studying the Renaissance:

Renaissance Hall of Fame

There are all sorts of hall of fames. For sports, music, motorcycles, inventions, etc. You have been charged with creating a hall of fame that represents the Renaissance. Your group will choose ten ideas from the Renaissance that will be inducted into the hall of fame. Decisions you will have to make.

- ♦ What makes it in? What doesn't?
- ♦ What long-term scientific, cultural, or social changes did it lead to?
- ♦ Why have you made the choices you have?

You will present these decisions to the class for consideration. You must also create an exhibition for the top three ideas and how it will be displayed in the hall of fame. Will be graded on the following three criteria:

- ♦ Presentation
- ♦ Content
- ♦ Display

Bonus Opportunity: Design the building/make a model of where the Hall of Fame will be housed based on Renaissance architecture and/or influence of other Renaissance ideas.

By students completing the project as is, they are covering the content standards they were required to learn. The bonus opportunity is merely an extra step, putting what they have learned into a more authentic product. Students would have to synthesize what they learned about the Renaissance through the project and construct a hall of fame that reflects this. I had students make theirs out of Legos, sugar cubes, or cardboard. As they presented their choices, they discussed how these would be displayed in the museum they made.

There were other projects where I used a single point rubric that looked like this:

	Shows progress	Shows mastery	Shows initiative
Product		Product meets the requirements of the learning objective and shows that the student has an understanding of it.	
Time Management		Turned in all materials by their deadline and paced self well, getting a little done every day.	
Quality		Product is of a good quality, showing that the student put effort into meeting the stated requirements.	

The idea behind this was to give students the opportunity to go above and beyond what was expected of them should they choose to. Many students chose just to show mastery in their projects, but there were some who pushed themselves to go deeper and show a greater understanding which was what its intentions were. Without this extra nudge, these students may not have challenged themselves, but with just a little guidance, they were willing to enrich themselves.

You can even use bonus opportunities on your assessments. For some of my assessments, I took to allowing students to choose which question they wanted to answer. I may present them with these three choices:

Choose 1 of these questions to answer (although feel free to answer as many as you like).

Name the Amendments in the Bill of Rights and what each of them does.

Explain how three of the Amendments from the Bill of Rights help to bring about freedom to Americans.

Pick one of the Amendments from the Bill of Rights you feel is the most important to our country. Justify why it is important with several real world examples to back your position.

These all essentially check for the same mastery; that students recognize what the Bill of Rights is and what it does. However, each question adds a little layer of understanding to it. In order to answer the second question, students not only have to know what they do, but how this helps citizens. The third question asks students to make an argument, justifying their answer with authentic examples, putting the Bill of Rights into the real world. A student who has just a basic understanding could choose to answer the first question, but a student who has a deeper understanding might consider the other two. One is not worth more than others, it is simply gauging how deep the student's understanding goes.

Because these scaffold into one another, a student could easily start by putting down the basics in the first response, adding more explanation of three of them in the second response, and then making an argument for which of these three is most important and for what reasons.

Here is another example of a bonus opportunity on an assessment.

Everything I know about this topic but wasn't asked on the test

What is light – energy that we can see

Luminous – things that give off light
      Examples: candles, light bulbs, sun, fire
      Non-luminous examples: moon, people, butter

Incandescent – heat and light
Fluorescent – electrical, UV light

Chemiluminescent – chemical reaction to visible light

Students learn a lot in a unit of study and the assessment can only capture so much of this mastery. Something really might have resonated with the student and yet was not asked on the assessment. This type of question allows the student to share what she learned but did not get the chance to show. It acknowledges the hard work she did in learning it and gives her space to display her understanding.

Where to Find Resources

Sometimes for bonus opportunities you can look to an above grade-level standard to see how far the student can take it. When I taught fifth-grade science, the learning standards looked like this:

Electricity

- ◆ Describe that electrical current in a circuit can produce thermal energy, light, sound and/or magnetic forces.
- ◆ Trace how electrical current travels by creating a simple electric circuit that will light a bulb.
- ◆ *Know there are many different ways to generate electricity, some which are more efficient than others.*
- ◆ *Surmise what your life would be like without electricity. How different would your life be and would you be able to function as you do now in your everyday life?*

The first two standards are the ones the fifth-grade curriculum called for. The third learning objective was taken word for word from the eighth-grade curriculum, while the final learning objective was one I created to try and get students to gain an awareness of how we use electricity every single day. I did not grade the final two learning objectives for mastery, but merely threw them out there to see what the students might do with them. I was usually pleasantly surprised at how much further they could take them and building upon the basics of what the grade level standards required.

You can also look to projects that match up with what students are learning and offer those as bonus opportunities. For example, if you are teaching the following learning objective:

Recognize that people must evaluate leaders to determine who is doing a good job.

You could teach the lesson as is, whether it be a discussion, students writing an essay, or a lecture. Then you might offer students the opportunity to expand their knowledge with a project such as this:

Presidential Place in History

Task

Choose a person who has served as President of the United States and answer the following question:

Does the President make history or does history make the President?

You will also determine whether you think this President did a good job or not and what evidence do you have to support this.

Product

Display your finding through one of the following:

♦ PowerPoint
♦ Paper
♦ Oral presentation
♦ Webpage

Outline

   I. Introduction
      a. Background Information
      b. When President?
      c. What was going on at the time in the United States/World?
   II. Presidency
      a. High points
      b. Low points
      c. Other interesting facts

(Continued)

III. Interpretation
  a. Effectiveness in a crisis
  b. Handling of economy/Domestic policies
  c. Foreign policies
  d. Leadership
  e. Popularity
  f. Role model
  g. Good or bad President?
IV. Importance in history
  a. How important was this President as compared to others?
  b. Could someone else have done a better job?
  c. Where would you place this person in importance to the forming of our country?
V. Conclusion
  a. Did history make the president or did the president make history?
  b. Summary of President and his accomplishment in history.

Students could then find a product they would be interested in producing either because they possess that skill already or they have always wanted to try it or get better at it.

What Impact It Will Have on Your Teaching/ Classroom

This bonus opportunity will have relatively little impact on your day-to-day teaching. Other than devising and offering the bonus opportunity, students would be independently working on these on their own. The only effort it would require on your part is evaluating the student's completed bonus opportunity, whether it be on the homework, on a project, or an assessment.

You want to be sure to provide feedback to students so that they know that their thinking was either right on target or a little off. This feedback should be specific rather than general or just awarding points. Providing this effective feedback is what makes this a 2 because it should take you a little bit of time to do this well.

How Much Work It Will Require of You to Successfully Execute It

Most of the work comes before and after. Before in the form of creating the bonus opportunity and what it might look like whether it be a question, a set of problems, or a project. After would be when you evaluate the student work and indicate what was done well, what needed further developed, and what could have been changed to make it better.

20time

Todd Talk Explaining the Strategy
https://youtu.be/2y0LOu4fvtk [2]

Overview of the Strategy

20time is a concept created by educator Kevin Brookhouser. He came up with the idea when he wondered what would happen if students were given creative freedom in the classroom, what would they choose to learn and what would they produce to show this learning? It is based on the Google 20% time. Google used to allow its workers 20% of their work time to dedicate to projects they were passionate and excited about, not ones they were assigned. These were projects that employees developed not as part of their work but as part of their desire to learn. Many Google products were developed during this allocated work time such as Gmail, Google Maps, and Google Talk. These innovative products came about because of the curiosity of the engineers.

Students are curious in the same way. From the moment they are born they are excited to learn new things including how to walk, talk, and eventually drive a car. Many times in school, this love of learning can get buried under work that the teacher assigns because he feels it is important, but students do not feel the same. What if we actually gave students the time to work on something they wanted to by providing a structure that they can use to learn about this?

What this looks like is you give students an allotted amount of time a day, or week, or even month, for them to work on their 20time project. You could give them 15 minutes every day. You could wait until the end of the week and give them an entire hour. You could decide to just do it once a month but devote an entire day to working on it. You can choose to assign the time however you choose, but you want to make sure you are consistent with it so that students know when to expect it so that they have the necessary materials to do their work. If you take too long between times working on it, students might forget what their 20time project was about or just lose their enthusiasm for it.

DOI: 10.4324/9781003238577-7

What It Looks Like in the Classroom

Typically the way a 20time project begins is students come up with a wicked problem. A wicked problem is an idea or problem that cannot be solved or if it can be solved, there are several different solutions that are possible, not just one right answer. Here are the characteristics of a wicked problem:

◆ Many times people do not know how they were made
◆ They have no fixed stopping point
◆ Solutions are not always right or wrong
◆ There is typically not a way to test the solution
◆ They are unique
◆ The problem might not be fully understood until a solution is worked on
◆ Just because you solve one aspect of the problem might cause another problem

Here are some common wicked problems:

Climate change	Healthcare	Pollution
Poverty	Equitable education	Social injustice
Natural disasters	Nuclear weapons	War

Then you challenge students to develop ways to help to solve these wicked problems. They can choose to tackle the entire problem such as the issue of poverty:

I want to look at the countries with the highest rates of poverty and determine what actions can be taken to help alleviate this.

Or students can attempt to break off a chunk of the problem and try to address that. Poverty has a lot of other contributing factors such as education, nutrition, healthcare, housing, crime, homelessness, and the economy. Students could decide to look into solutions for one of these more tangible problems:

I want to help people in my community who cannot afford it, to have food.

It is important to remember that even though the student should be passionate about the project, it is not a passion project. A passion project is about the person, 20time is about the problem. The problem is not even about doing good although that can be a bonus. Instead, this type of project is about developing the creative abilities one would need to take on a wicked problem.

For example, a student is concerned with the wicked problem of bullying. This is a difficult problem to attempt to solve with there certainly not being any one solution. The student may look at all sorts of options such as listed here:

♦ Create a mentoring program where older students help students who have either been bullied or have been accused of bullying
♦ Start an anti-bullying club
♦ Institute an awareness campaign with posters around the school and announcements over the school PA
♦ Have the school board create a clear definition of what bullying is so that teachers know how to enforce it
♦ Have a system that rewards students who are kind to others to incentivize them to be nicer

Ultimately, the student decides he wants to educate people about the issue and provide them with realistic solutions. Some ideas he brainstorms are listed here:

♦ Going to classrooms and giving a mini-lesson on what to do if you feel as though you are being bullied
♦ Developing curriculum that allows teachers to address the issue
♦ Using counselors and making sure they have proper training for how to help with a bullying issue
♦ Putting on a school assembly where they have skits that show what to do when someone is being a bully

The student decides to write and illustrate a children's book that will have the moral lesson of why you shouldn't bully and what you can do to prevent it. He asks the second-grade teachers in the district to read this book to their students during story time on Anti-Bullying Day, which is May 4. Much of his 20time is spent creating this book and then mass producing it so that teachers have enough copies.

As happy an ending as this situation might seem to have, keep in mind, some of these choices might not work for the student and he might need to rethink his project. This is not only perfectly fine, it is part of the learning process of 20time. That is why 20 time encourages wicked problems; so that students will go big, possibly fail, and learn how to reset themselves and move forward. This is how grit is developed and is especially important for gifted students who many times things come really easy to. So when they are faced with a challenge or something that does not have an easy answer, they may struggle. This helps them to develop coping mechanisms for what to do when they are not successful.

Because you are trying to solve a problem that does not seem to have a solution, students might not know exactly where they are going or how to get there. However, they will need a structure that helps in whatever journey students decide to take. This is one such structure:

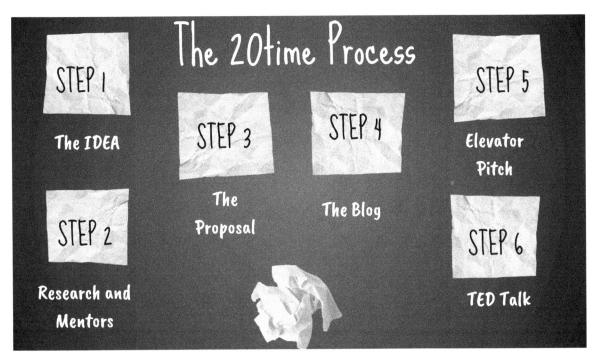

Step 1. Brainstorm: This has the students discovering issues they feel passionate about. During this time they also need to consider who their audience is going to be. This will help later when they decide what they are going to produce. Different students will progress through this at different paces. The important thing is to have graphic organizers in place to help focus their thinking. Here is one such example:

20time

Complete the suggestions below to help you to develop an idea for your 20time project.

I could build:

I could research:

I could talk to this person about my problem:

I could create this to solve a problem:

I could start a fundraiser by:

I could write:

I could use technology to:

I could develop a plan to improve…:

I could investigate:

I could solve:

Step 2. Research and Mentors: Students will need research on their chosen topic and become experts on it. This includes finding examples of what has been tried before and how successful each one was. It is also finding resources that will help students to generate their own ideas. Students will also reach out and try to find a mentor who carries a certain amount of expertise on the topic. For example, if you are looking at global warming, contact a professor at a local university who studies this. If you are looking at natural disasters, contacting someone at the Red Cross who deals with these or a weather expert if your natural disaster is caused by that. For a problem dealing with human rights, a student might hook up with the local chapter of Amnesty International who might be able to provide some insights.

Step 3. The Proposal: In order to focus students after their brainstorming and research steps, they must funnel their ideas into a proposal. This also allows you to get an idea of their plan so that you know how to support it. The downside of a wicked idea is that it is wicked hard to come up with a feasible solution that can be accomplished in the course of 12 weeks or even an entire schoolyear. He is a way they can organize their thoughts:

Proposal: [title of project]

[subtitle that helps describe the project]

Needs and Opportunities
Explain the problem you have noticed that needs to be solved with a project like yours. This is also your hook, so make sure you grab our attention.

Audience / Clients / Users
Explain who will benefit from your project. How will you be able to access them for an empathy interview?

Timeline
What is your monthly timeline for this project. I want to see a list of deliverables with deadlines. You may find that the timeline needs adjustment during the course of the year, which may be fine. Check in with me if that's the case.

September 1 Deliverables	
October 1 Deliverables	
November 1 Deliverables	
December 1 Deliverables	
January 1 Deliverables	
February 1 Deliverables	
March 1 Deliverables	
April 1 Deliverables	
May 1 Deliverables	

Product
What is the actual product you will show this spring. This project may be made of atoms or bits, but you must have something to show. I'm not interested seeing a bunch of great ideas at the end of the year. I want to see things.

Reality Check
I am looking for moonshots here, but even moonshots need budgets. What equipment are you going to need? What other capital expenditures do you anticipate, and how will you meet them?

Conclusion
Wrap it up. Why are you fired up about this project? Inspire us to support you, and give us a great reason to approve your project.

A document like this proposal allows students to see how the work will be done and gives them a sense of attainability. After planning out how they intend to accomplish this feat of solving the wicked problem, students must present it to you for your approval.

Step 4. The Elevator Pitch: This involves students being able to explain their entire 20time project in only a minute or two. This forces students to focus their ideas even further and to be able to communicate it clearly to someone else.

Brookhouser lays out the parts of the elevator pitch in his book, *The 20time Project*:

1. Problem statement: Explain what the problem is, and why it's a significant problem.
2. It gets worse: Explain how failing to solve this problem could cause more problems.
3. Glimmer of hope: Suggest that the situation can get better.
4. The novel solution: Explain how a new idea can help solve the problem.
5. The credible authority: Demonstrate that you are the right person to solve it.
6. The vision: Inspire the audience by painting a picture of how (Brookhouser, 2015).

By doing this, students are also learning the valuable 21st-century skill of public speaking and persuasion. They could either present this to the class, to another authentic audience, or they could create a video of the pitch. Whichever is chosen, students must make it their goal to get someone interested in their idea.

Step 5. The Blog: This is a great way to keep track of where students are on a weekly basis rather than waiting until toward the end of the project when it is too late to make changes. For this, students write a blog of at least 150 words. They can do this on a Google doc or Word document. The purpose of this blog is for students to reflect upon their progress. You can use these three questions as guidance for students:

1. What did you accomplish this week?
2. What are you working on right now?
3. What do you plan to do next?

These then become fodder for conversation with students about their project, what they see as working, and what they need to do to improve. You can also get updates on how the work with their mentor is going.

Step 6. The final product at the end of the project will be a 5-minute TED Talk where students describe their project and reflect on what they learned. This should be given to an authentic audience such as having an evening of TED Talks with parents invited, having a group of the mentors from the project act as the audience, or streaming it for people to see. This is what a graphic organizer might look like to help students in writing their TED Talk.

Outline for Informative Speech
(remember, a 5-minute speech is typically 750 words long)

My idea I tried to solve:

Introduction

Opening Statement (how can you hook your audience by getting their attention):

Content (this should provide the audience with information as to what your idea was and why you had interest in):

Body

How did you attempt to solve your problem, your journey on this project?

Were you successful or not in solving your problem and why was this?

Do you think there will be a successful solution in the future?

What can we as an audience do to help with this problem?

Reflection

What was the most important lesson you learned from working on this project:

Closing statement (What can you leave the audience with to make your speech a memorable one):

Where to Find Resources

There are several resources for those working on a 20time project:

- ◆ http://www.20time.org/students (great video on what students can do with their project
- ◆ https://www.20timeineducation.com/20-project/20-time-template-series (provides several templates you can use to design your own 20time lesson)
- ◆ https://www.cultofpedagogy.com/20-time-ajjuliani/ (this is a podcast about how to do 20time)

◆ https://www.amazon.com/20Time-Project-educators-future-ready-innovation/
dp/1502305240/ref=sr_1_1?dchild=1&keywords=20time&qid=1621738108&sr=8-1
(if you are a Kindle Unlimited member you can read for free)
◆ https://laurarandazzo.com/tag/20time/ (several examples of 20time projects plus
good advice on how to run one)

In addition, Genius Hour, which is a program very similar to 20time, also has some good
resources including:

◆ https://geniushour.com/
◆ Genius Hour: Passion Projects that Ignite Innovation and Student Inquiry by Andy
McNair

A downloadable PDF of the graphic organizers and such shared in this chapter can be
found on my website at www.thegiftedguy.com/resources under 20time.

What Impact It Will Have on Your Teaching/
Classroom

The only affect 20time will have on your classroom is you deciding when you are going to
give students a time and space to work on it. It is not going to be used as part of your
regular curriculum nor should it be used as a means to take a grade. The whole point of
20 time is that it should not feel like school. Instead, it should be sparking that love of
learning that students already possess and not doing it for the sake of the points, but for the
sake of learning.

Here is a weekly schedule for a middle school teacher that shows what this time might
look like:

Monday	Tuesday	Wednesday	Thursday	Friday
8:30–9:55 – math	8:30–9:55 – math	8:30–9:55 – math	8:30–9:55 – math	8:30–9:55 – math
10:00–11:25 – ELA	10:00–11:25 – ELA	10:00–11:25 – ELA	10:00–11:25 – ELA	10:00–11:25 – ELA
11:25–12:25 – lunch/recess	11:25–12:25 – lunch/recess	11:25–12:25 – lunch/recess	11:25–12:25 – lunch/recess	11:25–12:25 – lunch/recess

(Continued)

Monday	Tuesday	Wednesday	Thursday	Friday
12:30–1:30 – specials (gym)	12:30–1:30 – specials (music)	12:30–1:30 – specials (art)	12:30–1:30 – specials (gym)	12:30–1:30 – specials (music)
1:35–2:35 – science	1:35–2:35 – social studies	1:35–2:35 – science	1:35–2:35 – social studies	1:35–2:35 – science or Social studies
2:40–3:20 STEM time	2:40–3:20 technology time	2:40–3:20 enrichment and intervention time	**2:40–3:20 – 20time**	2:40–3:20 – team clubs

How Much Work It Will Require of You to Successfully Execute It

Other than providing the time to work on their 20time projects, your role becomes more an advisor than a teacher. Because students should be passionate about the project either because it is something they care about or something they chose, student motivation should be fairly high for enrichment such as this. However, there will be times where there is a lull in the enthusiasm students have for the project. It looks something like this (provided by Laura Randazzo):

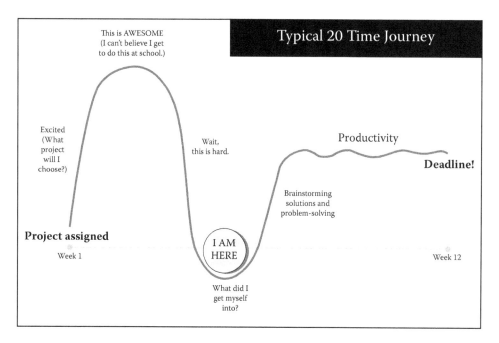

Your main role will be providing coaching and support when students do hit the low part of their workflow to get them back on track and finishing their project.

Mentors/Mentorship

Todd Talk Explaining the Strategy
https://youtu.be/1VTi8VdXUS0 [2]

Overview of the Strategy

Many times teachers are expected to know everything, to be the experts about their subject area or class and to have all of the correct answers. This of course is unrealistic. Even for a teacher who knows a lot about their chosen area of teaching, there are always other people out there who know more. And because of all of the material and curriculum to be covered in a year-long course, it would be impossible to know everything. This is where mentors and mentorships come into play. These are the experts you can use to help your students, you just need to know where to find them and how to connect them with your students.

This is especially important with gifted students who sometimes have a greater understanding of a topic than the teacher. Using these mentors can be helpful because they can take it to the next level and challenge students in a way you may be unable to.

What It Looks Like in the Classroom

This can look like a lot of things depending on what your needs are for your students. If you have a student in your gifted classroom who is really passionate about a topic and has become an expert herself, surpassing even your knowledge, you might want to find someone who is more of an expert to act as a mentor to this student. For example, a fifth-grade student of yours just loves robotics, taking your Lego Mindstorm sets and creating amazing robots with it. You have a decent understanding of robotics but because you are not using it all the time, it is fairly basic. You reach out to the robotics coach at the high school to see if he has any suggestions. He has a student on his team who is pretty advanced so between the two of you, you make arrangements for your student to attend a robotics practice and the coach makes sure to introduce your student to his. The older

DOI: 10.4324/9781003238577-8

student takes the younger one under his wing, showing him how they use the robotics, furthering your student's understanding. This mentorship continues throughout the school year, your student attending practices from time to time and using what he is learning to develop a robot of his own that is more advanced then he could have with just the Mindstorm set.

You could find a mentor for groups of students. When my students were working on Future City Competition, I reached out to the local university to see if there were any graduate students in the engineering department who would be willing to act as a mentor. Turns out they actually encouraged their grad students to do service such as this and were able to provide me with a dozen mentors, one for each of my groups. During the process, students never actually met face to face with their mentor. Questions were asked through email and answered by the graduate students. Occasionally they would get on a Google Meet to show the mentor what they were working on, receiving feedback on what could be better. When we finally had the showcase event where students displayed their future city, I extended an invitation to all of the mentors to attend which many of them did. This was great because I myself am not an engineer. Having these experts who are studying to be one brought a lot to my students' cities.

Other times you might want to find mentors that can help each of your students. If you were having students write a memoir where they are sharing an important part of their life and what it means to them, you might want to contact your state's writers' guild or reach out if there are ones in the area to see if members would be willing to be a writing mentor. Students would give drafts of their memoirs to these mentors or workshop their pieces, receiving advice on how to make the writing better and have phone conversations when needing ideas for techniques to use. These mentors can provide your students a much more personalized instruction that you can to 30 some students.

The are also mentorships. This is when students go experience what an expert goes through on a daily basis. This mentorship might be short-term, it might last longer. I assigned a research paper where students investigated a career they were interested in pursuing as an adult. Part of the process required them to interview someone in their field of interest and to ask questions that an expert such as this would be able to answer. As a bonus, I suggested to students that they ask their mentor if they could shadow them for a day or so to see what went on in such a career. I had a student who went to a veterinarian office and shadowed his working with animals for the day. I had a student who wanted to be a teacher who asked a former teacher of hers if she could come spend the day with her to get an idea of what a day in the life of a teacher looked like. I had a student who wanted to be a hairdresser and so worked with a local hairdresser to get an idea of what went on in a job such as this. These mentorships were more valuable than anything these students could have read in a book or seen in a video. It was firsthand real-life experience that gave them a glimpse of what their life might be life should they pursue such a career.

We had our students participate in a longer mentorship where they worked with someone for months, not a single day. This is what the project looked like:

Christopher Program Seniors

Political Action Project

Goal of the Project
To *implement* a project that elicits *social change* through *political action*.

Steps of the Project
1. Students will identify an issue through a six-week fieldwork carried out two days a week.
2. From the fieldwork, an issue will be identified and students will develop a plan to create change for this issue.
3. Students will then have an additional six weeks to carry out their plan using political action.

Parameters of the Project
♦ Must be lasting change
♦ Systemic change
♦ Affect many people
♦ Multi-faceted (attack problem in many ways)

Project Essential Knowledge, Skills, and Attitudes

Essential Knowledge	Essential Skills
Legislative Process	Persuasive speech/writing
Federalism	Networking
Historical cases of citizen action	Communication skills
Special Interest Group tactics	Observation & analysis of fieldwork
Power of the Press	Analysis of non-fiction texts

Essential Attitudes
INDIVIDUALS HAVE POWER
THE "LITTLE GUY" **CAN** MAKE A DIFFERENCE
IT IS WORTH IT TO AIM HIGH

Methods
Throughout the project, students will engage in several different types of learning experiences:

(*Continued*)

♦ Research projects and presentations
♦ Fieldwork with groups or institutions that are affected by political issues
♦ Panel presentations with members of press, lobbyists, and political activists
♦ Field trips and meetings with local and state political figures
♦ Weekly "critical friends group" meetings with classmates to compare and analyze learnings that have occurred during the fieldwork
♦ Text-based discussions on articles or chapters dealing with issues of government and social change

Fieldwork
Each student will set up and conduct six weeks of fieldwork at a setting in which he or she can learn more about a chosen political issue. The work may be at a place in which policy is made (i.e., the statehouse), influenced (i.e., a special interest group/lobbyist), or carried out (i.e., a public school). The fieldwork will be done for six weeks on Wednesdays and Thursdays during class time.

We had a unique situation where we worked with seniors who came to our program from around the county so they had transportation that could get themselves to their mentorships the two days a week they needed to be there. Students arranged mentorships with political party headquarters, local government offices, schools, lawyers and judges, the State House, and others. During this six weeks, they learned more about how government worked than anything we could have taught them in the classroom. They got to experience for themselves how it works in the real world and more importantly, learned what they can do to be a part of the process of bringing about real change. This was not something we could have hoped to replicat within the classroom walls. This experiential learning was far more powerful and relevant than anything we could have created.

Where to Find Resources

Depending on the age of your students, older students are always an easy place to start. Connecting elementary students with middle schoolers or middle schoolers with high schoolers and even high school students with college ones. Much like the young Albert Einstein who had an older mentor named Max Talmey, this older student can act as a role model and inspiration which causes them to achieve great feats.

Another great place to look is at nearby universities. It may take you a few phone calls or emails to find the correct person, but many times, they are eager to help in any way they can. Look for people in community outreach, advisors for graduate students, and if you know what you are looking for, contact professors directly.

I once had a fifth-grade girl who was doing a project on soil sampling. She called a professor at The Ohio State University and somehow arranged for a conversation with this expert mentor. Her mother drove her down to his office one day after school and he kindly gave her two hours of his valuable time to answer her questions and help with her project. A few months later we were watching the documentary *An Inconvenient Truth*, which is the Al Gore lecture on the dangers of global warming. There was a scene where there were scientists in the Artic taking ground samples. They interviewed one of these scientists for the documentary and my student shouted out, "Hey, that's the guy who met with me". This guy, who was an internationally renowned expert on his given topic was willing to take some time and work with an 11-year-old. The point is, university people are teachers too and often times they want to help students any way they can.

You can turn to professional organizations such as guilds. There are guilds for many professions such as architects, lawyers, engineers, writers, artists, educators, medical, and even herbalists. Many of these organizations already have programs in place where they offer their services as mentors. You just have to connect with the organization and make arrangements.

What Impact It Will Have on Your Teaching/ Classroom

Because most of this work will be done outside of the classroom, there will not be a large effect on your classroom practices. In fact, these mentors with be of great help because they are taking some of the heavy load off of your shoulders and giving you a hand in teaching them.

How Much Work It Will Require of You to Successfully Execute It

Depending on the age of your students, your main role will be having to possibly help students to arrange the mentorship or setting them up altogether. There is something to be said about having students, even young ones, arrange for their own though. If you decide to try this route, there are a few skills you would want to teach them to ensure success. One of these might be how to make a professional phone call. I used this lesson with my students:

Making a Phone Call

◆ Within 60 seconds, people will make assumptions about one's education, background, ability, and personality based on their voice alone.

♦ What type of impression is your "phone" voice making? Indeed there are two areas you should be aware of when speaking. One is "what" you say, the other "how" you say it.

♦ Studies show that as much as 87% of the listener's opinion of you is based on your voice alone. That leaves only 13% allocated to what we are saying to make a positive impression. With numbers like these it is easy to see why your voice is so important.

  • Be Prepared: Be aware of what you are going to say BEFORE making the call. Then practice and rehearse.
  • Professional Greeting: Remember the 87% rule above and make a good impression.
  • Prepare and Then Answer: Have a notepad and pen by your phone at all times. Write down the caller's name and use it during the conversation.
  • Be an Active Listner: Take notes, ask for correct spelling, and so forth.
  • Promptly Return Calls: Set a goal to return phone calls within 4 hours, it will make a positive statement about you and your image.

If You Leave Messages for Others Remember These Tips

♦ Slow Down: Don't speak too fast. Slow down when you are leaving a message, especially if you have an accent. If you make your message hard to understand or if the listener has to replay it several times to get your message your reputation is slipping in their mind.

♦ Clearly Say Your Name: Make absolutely sure the caller will understand your name. Consider spelling your name if hard to pronounce or is not a common name.

♦ S-L-O-W Down: When leaving your phone number go slow. Most likely the listener is writing down your number, make it easy for them to do so. Repeat the number. Consider saying your number at the beginning and end of your voice mail. People will appreciate this.

♦ Leave Your Name and Reason for Calling: Leave the listener with all the information they will need to know about you. Don't make them guess. Always leave the reason you are calling. It is very unprofessional to just leave a message simply saying "give me a call".

♦ Make It Easy for Them to Return Your Call: Tell them a good time to return your call. Give them a date, time, and phone number.

♦ Be Professional: People do judge you by the tone of your voice. Increase your image by sounding professional in everything you do over the phone:
  • Figure out who you are going to call about being your mentor.
  • Then sit down and write out what you are going to say.
  • Once you have done this practice making the call with a partner and have them practice with you as well.
  • Your goal over the next couple of days is to call someone and ask them to be your mentor.

Another would be setting expectations for how to behave when working with a mentor. Some things to consider are as follows:

- Take the initiative in the relationship. Invite your mentor to meet with you, suggest topics to discuss, ask for what you need. Use email, phone, and time in person.
- Bring questions, confusions, concerns, and problems. But also bring successes, alternatives, and ideas. See your mentor as someone who can help you be you.
- Meet as often as is appropriate. Scheduling in advance, spontaneity, and a combination are all fine – as long as they work with you both. Make sure you call or show up on time.
- Don't expect your mentor to know everything or be able to help in every situation. But do check with your mentor early on when you need help.
- Ask for information and, if appropriate, advice. Understand that any advice is not the last word, and may not be right for you. The more important a concern, the more important to weigh advice carefully and get second and third opinions.
- Be open to discussions and constructive alternative ways to handle tasks.
- Elicit a mentor's help in developing other informal supportive relationships.
- Be honest about any minor concerns regarding the mentoring relationship. If things are just not working, you can get a new mentor.

You might want to make sure you communicate with the mentor and set the level of expectation on their end. Some of these expectations might be:

General Responsibilities of Mentors

1. **Advising:** The mentor responds to a student's need to gain information needed to carry out a task effectively.
2. **Communicating:** The mentor works consistently to ensure that open lines of communication are always available.
3. **Counseling:** The mentor provides needed emotional support to a student.
4. **Guiding:** The mentor works to acquaint a student to the informal and formal norms of a particular system.
5. **Modeling:** The mentor serves as a role model by consistently demonstrating professional and competent performance.
6. **Skill developing:** The mentor assists the student in learning skills needed to carry out their task effectively.
7. **Professionalism:** Remember that these are children and you are a mentor they are looking up to. Please carry yourself with the upmost professionalism to set a good example for them.

You also will have to make sure that students have permission to take part in a mentorship. This should be run through the school and with their parents to make sure everyone knows what is going on. Some schools might even require a background check or a volunteer certificate from central office. You will want to do your due diligence and make sure of the procedures for your district and school.

Independent Projects

Todd Talk Explaining the Strategy
https://youtu.be/G47Nl0_jCLE [2]

Overview of the Strategy

Independent projects are an option for students who have shown they have already gained mastery of the lesson you are about the teach. It allows a student to explore something in more depth or to learn something they are curious about. The teacher can determine the requirements of the independent project. For instance, when I was teaching science, if a student tested out of a unit of study, they were allowed to do an independent project on anything they were interested in as long as it was tied to science. I had students choosing to learn about the physics of rollercoasters, the best launch angle for a batter to use in order to hit a homerun, the evolution of birds and how they came from dinosaurs, and an effective way for us to produce electricity without harming the environment. I told students right upfront, I would not be using these independent projects as a grade. I had already put an A in the grade book when they demonstrated mastery on the pre-assessment. I would however provide them with feedback on the project. What was remarkable about this is that even though it was not attached to a letter grade, students worked much harder on their independent projects than they did the projects that I assigned. This was because they were learning about something they were interested in based on the fact that they chose it.

What It Looks Like in the Classroom

Depending on how you set it up, what it looks like in most cases is while the rest of the class is going through the lessons and activities you have created, the student working on the independent project works, well, independently. You as the teacher are there to support her, answering questions and providing resources, but the student does most of this work her own. That means the student might be off in the corner with her earbuds, watching an educational video that informs her about her topic. Or she could be on the floor creating her Styrofoam model that she is making to display what she has learned. Depending on your school setup, you might write her a pass to the media center or technology lab so that she

DOI: 10.4324/9781003238577-9

can research or work on her product with the proper resources. Just know that she will not be doing what everyone else is doing. She is figuring out how to learn independently, which means she should not be asking questions every few minutes or pulling your attention away from the rest of the class all of the time.

Where to Find Resources

I typically have three tools that I use with students who are going to be working on an independent project. They are (1) student contract, (2) calendar, (3) rubric. Students cannot begin the independent project without these three items in place because they serve as the backbone of the work.

A student contract looks like this:

Project Contract

Student(s) Name: _____

Project Topic: _____

Essential Question:

Due Date of Project:

Learning Outcomes *(at least three)*:

Group Goal(s): _____

_____

_____

Product of Project: _____

_____

_____

Student(s) Signature: _____

_____

_____

_____

Teacher Signature: _____

What this does is allows students to look at the big picture of what they are going to be learning and then break it down into parts. They first start by creating learning objectives. If a student says he wants to learn about caves, that is not a learning objective, that is a topic. What specifically does the student want to learn about caves? He would have to turn this into learning objectives that can be answered and evaluated. For instance, after doing some initial research, the student might come up with these learning objectives:

◆ What are some ways that a cave is formed?
◆ What are some ecosystems that are found in caves and how does their food chain work?
◆ What are some of the advantages to exploring caves? Why would you explore a cave?
◆ What is a cave you were interested in and what features caused you to be impressed by it?

This provides the student a compass of where to take the learning. Depending on the child, he might need some guidance as to what a learning objective looks like. Some general rules are as follows:

◆ Should not be able to be answered in a single word or sentence
◆ Should not just be facts but display some thinking as well
◆ Should be a mix of lower and higher level objectives
◆ Should all be linked to the topic
◆ Should be able to be backed by evidence, even an opinion

Students might be learning other skills by working on this project such as research, interviewing, technology, initiative, or productivity. They would indicate that under skills.

You can see there is a section where students need to put their product. You can set your contract up however you want, but I wanted students to choose what the end product was going to be before they even began the project. This would give them something to work toward and allow them to collect the evidence they need to support it. For the cave project, the student might determine that he is going to create a model of a specific cave, and, indicate how it was formed, labeling the different parts of the ecosystem, giving the history of how the cave became well-known, and other features that impressed the student. Notice that this product allows the student to demonstrate all four of the learning objectives. If the student had chosen instead to make a video giving us a tour of a local cave, it might have been difficult to get all of the learning objectives into this product.

Just because the student is working independently does not mean they have unlimited time. You would determine how much time the student would have for the project, for example, two weeks. Then the student would have to plot out on the calendar what they need to do during this two weeks in order to produce something that demonstrates mastery. This does a few things:

1. Allows them to see the big picture of the project and how they can attain mastery
2. Allows them to plot out their project so that they have something to guide them
3. Allows them to prioritize, learning time management skills

I give them a blank calendar such as this:

Day____	Day____	Day____	Day____	Day____
Day____	Day____	Day____	Day____	Day____

Then the student determines the steps that need to be done to accomplish his end product and how much time he is going to give for each step. In the case of the cave project, the student needs to figure out the steps he will need to complete to get to his final product of the model of the cave. He might break it down like this:

Step 1. Research how caves are formed

Step 2. Research ecosystems commonly found in caves

Step 3. Find some advantages to exploring caves

Step 4. Identify and research a cave that I find interesting

Step 5. Design model of cave

Step 6. Determine supplies am going to need

Step 7. Build model

Step 8. Label model

This would enable him to achieve his final product with everything he needs to demonstrate mastery. He then takes these steps and determines how much time spent for each, budgeting his time out over the two weeks he has been given. It might be spread out like this:

Table 9.1

Day 1 Research how caves are formed	Day 2 Research various ecosystems found in caves	Day 3 Find advantages of exploring and identify a cave I want to make a model of	Day 4 Draw design of model based on the cave I have chosen	Day 5 Finish design of model and list supplies needed to build
Day 6 Begin to build model	Day 7 Continue to build model	Day 8 Finish building model	Day 9 Label parts of model	Day 10 Double check to make sure all learning objectives addressed in model and labels

The student determines for himself how he will spend his time. The calendar is not written in stone, but it does give the teacher and student something to talk about when checking in on the project. Where is the student on the calendar and is he where he wants to be? Here is a Todd Talk to provide more information on how to create a student calendar https://youtu.be/z8FHraHxKDU.

A final piece to the puzzle would be the creation of the grading rubric. As I stated before, I never put a grade in the grade book for independent projects, but I did evaluate the student's work and provide both written and verbal feedback for what I thought was done well and what could have been improved. Since this is their project, I had students create a rubric for how it was to be evaluated. This put them in charge of their learning and how it would be determined if they had mastered this learning. I gave them a blank rubric, which looked like this:

Project Rubric

Overall			
Excellent			
Good			
Needs Improvement			

They were to determine what the major aspects of the project were and what they looked like at various levels of mastery. For example, in the cave project, the student would look at all of the aspects of the product that show mastery:

♦ Content
♦ Model
♦ Research

He would then need to show what this looks like when done well in addition to not so well. A finished rubric might look like this:

Table 9.2

	Content	**Model**	**Research**
Excellent	♦ Successfully explains all learning objectives with clear examples and detail ♦ Includes not just facts but student insight and analysis showing a full understanding.	♦ Model gives a representation of what the cave looks like and the many specific features it has. ♦ Model has labels that show with much detail information about the cave.	♦ Statements and opinions are backed with well researched examples. ♦ Research is from multiple, reputable sources (need bibliography).
Good	♦ Successfully explains all learning objectives but places where clear examples and detail are needed more ♦ Includes not just facts but also student insight and analysis, but not always showing a full understanding.	♦ Model gives a general representation of what the cave looks like but does not include many specific features it has. ♦ Model has labels that give general information but not enough detail about the cave.	♦ Statements and opinions are backed with researched examples but need more to make point. ♦ Research is from multiple sources but some not reputable (need bibliography).
Needs Improvement	♦ Does not explain all learning objectives with clear examples and detail.	♦ Model does not give a very good representation of what the cave looks like, not	♦ Statements and opinions are not backed with researched examples.

(Continued)

Table 9.2 (Continued)

	Content	Model	Research
	◆ Includes just facts and not much student insight and analysis.	pointing out any or very few of its features. ◆ Model does not have labels that include information about the cave or they are wrong.	◆ Research is either from just couple of sources or ones that are not reputable (need bibliography).

This would both give the student standards of quality that he needs to achieve, and gives the teacher a clear idea of how to evaluate the student's work. For steps to how to create an objective rubric, you can watch this Todd Talk https://youtu.be/H_eGyATb4JA.

It is the combination of these three tools that will help the student to stay on task in his independent work and give the teacher guidance on how to mentor the student and help him should he become stuck. You can get blank copies of the contract, calendar, and rubric as well as steps for students to create their rubric by going to my website https://www.thegiftedguy.com/prof-development. These are all under the topic of Tools for Independent Projects.

What Impact It Will Have on Your Teaching/ Classroom

If set up correctly, there will be very little for you to have to do during your class, hence the idea of an independent project. Students might need some guidance at the beginning in creating the tools for their independent project, with the occasional check-in to support students, but conceivably a student could do this work autonomously while you are working with the rest of the class on the general lesson. I had one sixth-grade student in particular who tested out of five of my six units of study, and by the time he was on his third project, I knew I could leave him on his own to product a high-quality product that showed me what he had learned, and he knew he could ask me questions should he need any help. I was not ignoring this student, but rather providing him with the space to learn valuable skills for how to learn on his own. This is the place where you want to get these students, where they become independent learners who do not need someone else to show them the way. They are able to create their own path. (By the way, the student did all five of his projects on the study of birds which was a passion of his. He is know employed as a naturalist, studying birds.)

How Much Work It Will Require of You to Successfully Execute It

Most of the work for the teacher comes at the beginning when you are helping students to set up their project. They might need some guidance on the learning objectives, how to divide their time on their calendar, and how to evaluate it on their rubric. Once a student is trained in this however, the next time he works on an independent project the teacher will not have to be as involved.

Although the student will be working independently, it will require you to conference with her every once in a while. This could be a brief check in to gauge where she is at and if she is struggling. It could be a fact check to make sure she is getting the proper information to complete her project. The best conversation to have though is the one where you listen to what she is trying to accomplish and provide encouragement to dig deeper or challenge herself through the process. This is where you challenge your gifted students, not by giving them harder work, but by getting them to think about something in a different way and consider the possibilities.

Pre-assessment

Todd Talk Explaining the Strategy
https://youtu.be/m2lHbtG9Ggg [3]

Overview of the Strategy

Before a student even begins a lesson in your class, how much do they already know? With some gifted students, it can be a lot. They may already be at the point that you want all students to end up at when you finish your lesson. Imagine you are a student who already knows how to multiply two-digit numbers, and you must go through all of the basic steps, work on problems you can easily solve, and go at the pace of the other students who are just trying to gain a basic understanding of how to multiply single-digit numbers. That would be really tough to sit through.

What if instead, we could try to determine what a student already knows? The problem is a lot of teachers give the student a pre-assessment, the students aces it, and the teacher makes the student go through the lesson anyway, knowing full well that the student already had mastery before they even began. I have had teachers say to me, "I doesn't hurt for them to learn it again", but that is where they are wrong. You have to think of the gifted child in this situation as suffering from what is known in economics as opportunity cost. Opportunity cost is not what you actually lost, it is what you could have gained but did not have the opportunity to do so. By the student having to go through something she has already learned, it cost her the opportunity to have learned something new and to have growth.

What we should do when a student has shown how much she knows already, is to begin her lesson there? Then she would be able to take it from that point and grow even more as a learner. This does take a certain amount of classroom management, because different students are going to be at different places. But how do you assess them all the same (the answer of course being that you don't, you assess them individually)? This is what is known as differentiation and involves adapting the lesson to the abilities of the student. Pre-assessments are a great tool to gather data to figure out where students are at on the spectrum of learning.

DOI: 10.4324/9781003238577-10

What It Looks Like in the Classroom

There are various types of pre-assessments you can use with students. Some of them are listed here:

♦ **Anecdotal records**: These are notes about student knowledge, skills, and behaviors. The teacher makes notes indicating what she observes and then uses the notes to determine the focus of the learning opportunities.

♦ **Anticipation guide**: It is used to activate students' prior knowledge and build curiosity about a new topic. Students are asked to anticipate what they think is going to happen in a book, or how they believe a science experiment will turn out, or how they think a math problem will play out.

♦ **Brainstorming**: This is usually just a knowledge dump, getting students to write everything they know about whatever topic you are going to be teaching. This might come in the form of word clouds, it could be lists, it could be freewriting where students write more a stream of consciousness. This can be activated by a writing prompt or simply by writing the topic on the board.

♦ **Concept maps**: Students are asked to create a map of ideas that are connected with a topic. They will use lines or linking words to join these concepts together. This shows that they get the connections.

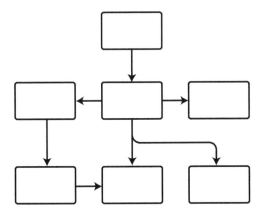

♦ **Discussion**: This is a verbal assessment of what a student may already know. Depending on how involved they are in the discussion and how in-depth their responses are might indicate this student has a good understanding. For example, you are going to be teaching about light in science class and you ask the class about the seven types of light rays and an example of where they might see it in the real world.

♦ **Entrance cards**: Similar to an exit card but you give it to students before starting the lesson to determine their prior knowledge. On an index card or half sheet of paper, students answer a small number of questions covering the learning targets for the next lesson. For example, if you are going to be teaching students the five-paragraph essay, you might want to see how much your students already know. You might have an entrance card that looks like this:

What are the parts of the five-paragraph essay and what purpose do they serve:
   1.
   2.
   3.
   4.
   5.

♦ **Inside-outside circles**: You divide the class into two equal groups. One forms a circle in the middle of the classroom. The second group then forms a circle around this so that they are face-to-face. The teacher provides a question or a topic and the person in the inside circle talks about what he or she knows about this for the allotted time. The teacher then tells pairs to switch, and the person in the outer circle gets his chance. Then the teacher asks the outer circle to rotate one spot to the right, and with a new partner they discuss another question/topic. The teacher moves around the room during this process and notes which students seem to know what they are talking about or can talk about it at great length.

♦ **Interviews**: This would be a one-on-one conversation with a student where the teacher talks with him about what he already knows about an upcoming topic. An example would be if the teacher plans a lesson concerning negative numbers and asks the student if he knows if there are any numbers below zero. This interview would allow the teacher to get a good idea of whether the student grasps the concept or not.

♦ **Journals**: These are done either in a notebook or on a computer document. Students are provided with a prompt and then asked to journal about it. A teacher might be getting ready to start a unit on the Civil War. He or she might provide a prompt such as this:

   Write about the major issue between the South and the North in the Civil War? What were some minor issues that were also causing the nation to be divided?

♦ **KWL charts**: Teacher use a chart to determine
   • K – What does the student know already?
   • W – What does the student want to know?
   • L – What does the student want to learn?

KWL		
What I Know	What I Want to Know	What I Learned

♦ **Most difficult first**: If a teacher is starting a lesson on a topic, she gives students the five most difficult questions she intends to ask through the course of it and sees how the students respond to them. This could be five questions dealing with square root and cubed root to determine whether students understand the concept. If students miss them all, they have been exposed to it. If a few are able to get a majority of them correct, maybe the teacher begins the unit a little further with that group.

♦ **One-minute essay**: Students are given a question about the new unit of study and are allowed to spend one minute answering it to the best of their ability. How quickly they are able to explain it or how much they are able to write in that minute might be an indicator that a particular student already possess a level of mastery. You might ask them:

You have one-minute to explain what you know about renewable resources.

♦ **Pre-test**: This is a written exam, could be a multiple-choice, short answer, and so forth, that mimics the summative assessment you plan to give students at the end of the lesson. If a student scores very well on it, the question becomes whether this student would need to go through the unit of concepts they already seem to know?

♦ **Self-evaluations**: This asks students to assess themselves. Although you can use a self-evaluation for content, I prefer to use them for skills because this helps students to develop a self-awareness about their abilities. Here is one I might give to students prior to engaging in research for a project:

1. On a scale from 1–5, 5 being expert level, how would you rate your ability to find information you need on the internet?
2. On a scale from 1–5, how comfortable are you in taking notes on the information that you find?
3. On a scale from 1–5, how do you rate your ability to tell a reputable source from one that is not as reputable?
4. On a scale from 1–5, how skilled are you at offering analysis of the research you plan to use?
5. On a scale from 1–5, how well do you find information from multiple sources that bring in different perspectives on the topic?

If students score high on this, I might allow them to independently work. If they are on the low end, I would work with them one-on-one or in small groups to develop the skills. I would of course follow this up with teacher observation to gauge for myself if they are as skilled as they indicated.

♦ **Surveys**: These are less about content and more about how a student feels about a topic or skill. It doesn't give you a completely accurate pictures of what a student can do, but it does show you how they think they can do. It is important to determine this mindset and whether the student believes he can be successful. This is an example of a survey designed to get an idea of how a student feels about math in general:

Mathematical MindsetCheck the Box That Best Describes How You Feel about These Statements.	Agree	Mostly Agree	Mostly Disagree	Disagree
1 You are born with your math ability.				
2 Your intelligence means you will be good at math.				
3 You have to be able to memorize to be good at math.				
4 Learning new math is more difficult than changing your math ability				
5 Your grade is a good indication of your math ability.				
6 You can improve your ability to understand math.				
7 How quick you are shows good math ability.				
8 You have to practice math in order to be good at it.				

♦ **Teacher observations**: You spend an entire year (or more) with these students and if you are paying attention, you get a pretty good understanding or what they can and cannot do. This time spent together acts as a performance-based assessment where students are demonstrating their abilities and skills and will give you a pretty good idea of what they are capable of and what they are able to do. This sort of informal pre-assessment can be made more objective with the use of a graphic organizer such as this:

Goals			Major tasks	Day 1	Day 2	Day 3	Day 4	Day 5	Day 6	Day 7	Day 8	Day 9	Day 10	Day 11	Day 12	Day 13	Day 14	Chad	Bonnie	Tracy	Ben	#5
			Complete contract/ Set goals	x														x	x	x	x	
			Research colony of New Jersey		x	x	x											x	x	x		
			Synthesize the research into bullet points				x														x	
			Create a rough draft of the brochure						x	x								x	x			
			Find maps/photos for use in the poster						x	x										x	x	
			Design a final draft on the computer of brochure								x	x	x	x	x			x	x			
			Get the posterboard								x									x		
			Print up photos/maps for use on poster								x										x	
			Create poster									x	x	x						x	x	
			Make sure poster from perspective of 1700s												x					x	x	
			Make sure brochure from perspective of 1700s												x			x	x			
			Use rubric to go over brochure													x		x	x			
			Use rubric to go over poster													x		x	x	x		

Goal #1: complete the project on time
Goal #2: get an A on the project
Goal #3: work together well

Project Deadline: January 25

Responsible Party — Group member #1: Chad; Group member #2: Bonnie; Group member #3: Tracy; Group member #4: Ben; Group member #5:

A teacher could put this on a clipboard and walk around the room, keeping track of student progress and having a record to look at later.

◆ **Writing samples**: Students create a collection of work throughout the year. These can be gathered in a portfolio or capstone, but this past work gives a teacher a good idea of what a student is capable of in regard to writing.

When I was a science teacher, I prepared pre-assessments for every unit of study. It was determining if a student already had mastered the major learning objectives, we were going to study throughout the course of the lesson. If a student scored 90% or higher, I simply gave them an A for the unit and gave them three choices:

1. They could take the topic they had just assessed out of and dig a bit deeper into it.
2. They could conduct an independent study concerning something else science related (independent studies is discussed in strategy nine.
3. They could choose anything they have wanted to learn about, didn't have to have anything to do with science, and create a project around that.

The one thing I never did that I see some teachers doing is put that student who has showed mastery with a student who is struggling, the thinking being that this advanced student could help the one having difficulty. This is one of the worst things you can do to a gifted child for a few reasons:

1. Just because someone has a good understanding of a topic doesn't mean they are able to teach this to someone who doesn't.
2. Often times gifted students do not suffer fools gladly, meaning they do not have the patience to work with someone who isn't getting it as quickly as they did.
3. The gifted child is not learning. He is merely going over information that he has already mastered. There is no growth for them.

These pre-assessments can be used to show a teacher that a student has already learned a concept, content, or skill, and may not need to go through the same lesson as others who still need to gain an understanding.

Where to Find Resources

Finding resources for a pre-assessment is similar to finding resources for assessments. You could find examples of pre-assessments through a Google search. I personally prefer to write them myself for a few reasons:

1. You can personalize the assessment to fit your students.
2. You can personalize the assessment to fit your particular curriculum.
3. You can personalize the assessment to fit a particular skill you want students to understand in addition to the content.

There are online assessments that can act as a diagnostic assessment that will provide you with information about your students and where they excel. Some that I have used in the past are Study Island, iReady, STAR, and IXL. I could then use this information to decide how to group students, who to accelerate, who had gaps, and other data to help me make informed decisions.

What Impact It Will Have on Your Teaching/ Classroom

This one is rated a 3 not because of the preparation or giving of the pre-assessment. It is what the teacher does afterward that affects your teaching/classroom. If a student shows that she already knows the material, this means that you will have to create an alternative plan for her. This might be a differentiated lesson where she is learning the same topic but merely at greater depth. It could mean creating an entirely different lesson for her. It might mean letting her create her own independent project, which was talked about in the last chapter. This does require some management skills, having most of the students working on one thing while a few select are doing something else.

How Much Work It Will Require of You to Successfully Execute It

As stated before, it just requires you providing the pre-assessment before beginning a lesson, assessing it for mastery, and deciding how to use the information you get from it. Most of the work is going to come after the results are in and you have students who have shown a propensity for being able to handle more than what you are planning to offer.

Performance Assessments

Todd Talk Explaining the Strategy
https://youtu.be/jdylxsoP_mk [3]

Overview of the Strategy

In the traditional classroom, the way things typically work is that students learn material and are then given a summative assessment to determine whether they have mastered said material. This assessment might come in many forms:

- Multiple-choice
- True/False
- Matching
- Fill-in-the-blank
- Short answer

What do all of these assessments have in common?

1. There is one correct answer
2. There are limitations to how much creativity students can show
3. They are mostly lower level thinking
4. There is a ceiling to them
5. There is no new learning going on, simply the recall of old

This is not good for gifted students (I would argue it is not good for any students) because it tells, not shows you what these students have learned. When students are *telling* the teacher what was learned, they are limited to what the teacher thinks should have been learned. When they *show* what was learned, they can take it as far as they are able to. They can also bring in skills and talents that were not explicitly taught in the lesson.

In order for gifted students to be able to show you what they learned, they need to have assessments where they have the room to do so. Performance assessments are a good alternative that allows students to find a conduit to show what they have learned at the level of mastery they have attained. According to the National Science Foundation science and engineering indicators (2016), performance-based assessments usually

DOI: 10.4324/9781003238577-11

 ◆ allow students to create their own response rather than to choose between several already created answers;
 ◆ are criterion-referenced, or provide a standard according to which a student's work is evaluated rather than in comparison with other students; and
 ◆ concentrate on the problem-solving process rather than on just obtaining the correct answer.

This allows for students to not only be creative, but encourages them to think big because they have no limit on what they can do. It also lets students play to their strengths. Case in point, I am awful at multiple-choice tests, even ones where I know the content. My mind starts racing when looking at the possible answers and I believe I can justify more than one. However, if you give me an essay, I can write on just about anything and make a convincing argument of my mastery of the topic. It allows me to harness my thinking and my creativity in order to show what I have learned. Similarly, if you have a student who is not a good writer but is excellent in discussion, why couldn't that student show you what he has learned by explaining it to you orally?

In addition, performance assessments have the advantage of the following:

 ◆ Direct Observations of Student Learning
 ◆ Good Instructional Alignment
 ◆ Interesting Assessments
 ◆ Instructional Feedback
 ◆ Measurement of Multiple Objectives and Concepts
 ◆ Active Student Learning
 ◆ Higher-Order Thinking Skills
 ◆ Student Interest and Empowerment
 ◆ Simulating real-world tasks that scientists, mathematicians, engineers, and researchers encounter
 ◆ Making the assessment authentic

What It Looks Like in the Classroom

What do performance assessments look like in the classroom? It means you provide students with other ways to demonstrate mastery. You might give them a couple of choices, you might give them a slew of choices, or you might just give them one but it is a different way of assessing them.

Sometimes you may use a performance assessment because it will show you a skill the students possess that a traditional test cannot. I always had my eighth graders write a research paper on westward expansion. I really didn't care if they remembered anything about their particular topic, but I did want them to know the basics of how to write a proper research paper. I had many students who came back to visit me from the high school who told me how ELA class was a breeze because they had already learned how to write a research paper in my class. In the end, this choice for a performance assessments was less about learning the content and more about learning the skill.

I typically had these choices for performance assessments in my class:

- ◆ **Journals/Student log**: Students could draw, write poetry, make lists, write letters from the perspective of another person, do charting, or have other possibilities to explore ideas.
- ◆ **Oral presentation**: A student sharing what he has learned in a verbal format. It usually involves an explanation with support to back this spoken thesis.
- ◆ **Role playing**: A form of creative oral presentation where a student must inhabit a specific person and carry out the role from that person's perspective.
- ◆ **Debate/Speech**: Another form of oral presentation but instead of seeking to inform, the main goal is to persuade.
- ◆ **Group discussion**: Allows students voice to feel as though they have some participation in the class.
- ◆ **Interview**: Student locates an expert in a topic he or she wants to know more about and conducts an interview where he or she gains valuable information.
- ◆ **Portfolio**: A student portfolio is a collection of materials that represents what a student learned.
- ◆ **Essay**: An essay asks a student to explain what he or she has learned in a formal written response.
- ◆ **Research paper**: Helps the student getting the information for himself using various sources. There is the process of finding, evaluating, and organizing the information.
- ◆ **Exhibition**: A product that shows what the student has learned, viewed by an authentic audience (Stanley, 2014).

Sometimes I would let students choose from these ten, sometimes I would shorten the list to just three or five, other times I did not give them a choice if I wanted them to be learning a particular skill such as public speaking or I wanted to get their reflection.

The nice thing about these is that if given a choice, students can choose assessments that allow them to demonstrate their skills and creativity. For example, if a student is really good at coding, he or she might be able to create a website that he can use to exhibit what he learned. This way he is learning the content as well as developing a skill he or she has interest in. This also can do wonders for motivating students. Even if they are not enamored with the content they are learning, they might be highly interested in the medium they are using to show mastery.

Another performance assessment that I liked to employ with my students was a capstone. I did these toward the end of the year and was typically a collection of their work that demonstrated their biggest a-ha's of the school year. They didn't necessarily have to be academic in nature or be tied to the content standards. It might be something they learned about themselves. This capstone acted as a reflection on what they had learned for the schoolyear and I felt it did a good job of showing their growth as learners. The important thing was the capstone was more for them than it was for me. It acted as a place where they could reflect upon what they do well, what still needs some work, and what they needed to do moving forward.

For more information on capstones, you can watch this Todd Talk https://youtu.be/SAX4vPW7MkU.

Where to Find Resources

What the performance assessment might look like will many times be determined by the students themselves. I usually just set basic parameters and they would then take it where they wanted. For example, I might tell them they have to do a visual presentation. They might choose to use PowerPoint, Google Slides, Prezi, or some other program to do this. How many slides and how to elaborate the animation would also be up to them. However, it is important to model for them what it can look like. These are some specific examples of what student products might look like:

♦ **Journals/Student log**: While reading The Hate U Give, a student decides to journal his feelings throughout the course of the book and how he would feel if in a similar situation.

♦ **Oral presentation**: In order to explain a mathematical concept such as integers, a student creates a video where he or she explains the basics of integers, and then works out problems on the board for people to see, explaining it step-by-step.

♦ **Role playing**: Student may play Julius Caesar for a living wax museum, dressing in a toga costume and speaking in first person about his many accomplishments as though he is Caesar.

♦ **Debate/Speech**: Students want to debate a new school policy of not allowing cell phones in the classrooms. They use the Lincoln-Douglas debate format. One side argues the benefits of being allowed to have your cell phone while the other side argues about the distractions it causes.

♦ **Group discussion**: Students were allowed to choose a book based on the theme of survival, forming five separate literary circles, each one discussing a different book. There is a group reading *Robison Crusoe, Lord of the Flies, Hatchet, The Stand*, and *The Martian*. Since the teacher cannot be at all of the discussions, the students lead it themselves, coming up with questions beforehand, and talking about specific instances in the text where they saw this theme of survival.

♦ **Interview**: When researching the job of a professional musician, a career he wants to pursue post high school, a student decides to interview a local musician to get direct responses to questions he may have about going into such a profession.

♦ **Portfolio**: A student has been keeping all of her assessments for math in a portfolio and analyzes her common mistakes she has made, demonstrating her growth as a learner and how she has carried this lesson into future assessments.

♦ **Essay**: A student writes a literary analysis essay comparing the transcendentalism themes found in both *Walden* and *Our Town*.

- ◆ **Research paper**: While studying the habitats of animals, a student writes a research paper where she learns about a river otter's habitat, how zoos construct their pens to simulate this, and what can be done to preserve their habitat in the wild.
- ◆ **Exhibition**: For science class, a student wishes to show the different properties of a solid and a liquid, so she makes a batch of oobleck while reading the Dr. Seuss book to the class.

I do have a book through Prufrock titled *Performance-Based Assessment for 21st-Century Skills* that provides all sorts of specific examples and more detailed explanations.

What Impact It Will Have on Your Teaching/ Classroom

This strategy will not necessarily affect the way you teach, but it will affect the way you assess. Because of this, it is a 3 on the classroom impact scale. It may also mean carving out time to allow students to give performances should they need to. Whereas if you give a whole class assessment, you might give students 45 minutes of class time to take this assessment. If you have ten students each needing to give a 10-minute speech, you will have to provide the class time for them to do so.

You don't have to start by giving kids tons of choices if you are just learning to use performance assessments. For the first few years I used them, I would dictate to students what assessment would be used for which unit. It wasn't until I got comfortable doing this that I began to give them more choice in the matter. I found this choice made for better products because students could choose something they were excited about.

One word of caution when using performance assessments. Try not to lay out every single requirement of the product. Otherwise students are not getting any intellectual or creative input, they are simply making widgets. You want to be a little more open with the requirements and see what students do with it. When I began to do this, I was amazed by what students would come up with.

How Much Work It Will Require of You to Successfully Execute It

The main work for performance assessments is determining how you will evaluate them. Typically this comes in the form of a rubric. You can either create these rubrics for yourself, or if you are allowing students to choose individually which assessment they will use to show mastery, students can make them themselves. No matter who makes them, they will need to be descriptive enough so that whatever is being evaluated can be done so objectively. If you are too general with the description, they subjectivity can work itself into the evaluation.

Take this general rubric concerning an oral presentation for instance:

CATEGORY	4	3	2	1
Posture and Eye Contact	Stands up straight, looks relaxed and confident. Establishes eye contact with everyone in the room during the presentation.	Stands up straight, and establishes eye contact with everyone in the room during the presentation.	Sometimes stands up straight and establishes eye contact.	Slouches and/or does not look at people during the presentation.
Preparedness	Student is completely prepared and has obviously rehearsed.	Student seems pretty prepared but might have needed a couple more rehearsals.	The student is somewhat prepared, but it is clear that rehearsal was lacking.	Student does not seem at all prepared to present.
Speaks Clearly	Speaks clearly and distinctly all (100-95%) the time, and mispronounces no words.	Speaks clearly and distinctly all (100-95%) the time, but mispronounces one word.	Speaks clearly and distinctly most (94-85%) of the time. Mispronounces no more than one word.	Often mumbles or can not be understood OR mispronounces more than one word.
Content	Shows a full understanding of the topic.	Shows a good understanding of the topic.	Shows a good understanding of parts of the topic.	Does not seem to understand the topic very well.

There are several problem with this.

♦ **Many of the adverbs used are very vague**: Look at the Content aspect. It describes it as a full understanding versus a good understanding. What exactly is the difference? Where is the line drawn between full and good? What does good even look like?

♦ **Would force the teacher to pay attention to things that would distract from other things that have more value**: When you look at posture and eye contact, it requires the grader to watch the posture of the speaker the entire time as well as whether he or she makes eye contact with every single person in the room. Although these are important aspect of public speaking, if the teacher is paying so much attention to this, they are not paying enough attention to the content students are presenting.

♦ **Does not show what many of these would actually look like**: When looking at the Preparedness, is uses the description "pretty prepared" to score a 3. What does pretty prepared look like? Does it mean putting on your best clothes and grooming yourself? Probably not, but there are no descriptions to indicate what the evaluator should be looking for or what they will see if the student accomplishes this.

♦ **Would allow other aspects to inflate the grades than actually show mastery**: Basically what a student could do with this rubric is have great posture, rehearse, and speak clearly, and he or she will at least get a 75%. The content could be misleading or completely wrong, and the student could still be given credit for mastery. That means the public speaking aspects are worth 3/4 of the grade, while the meat of the presentation, the content, is only 1/4.

♦ **Is too specific with some of the language**: Although you should be specific with your descriptions, if you are too specific, this can be a problem. Look in the Speaks Clearly section. It asks that students speak clearly 95% of the time, but if they mispronounce one word, they go from a 4 to a 3. That is a lot to ask. It is basically requiring the student to be perfect in order to get a 4. Not only that, if a student speaks clearly 85%–95% of the time, they get a 2. That means the student did a good job but they are only getting half of the points. This is not to mention that I do not even know what 85% of the time looks like.

A rubric such as this, which was created by an online program which a lot of teachers use, does not show the students what they must do in order to achieve mastery. It is too vague. In addition, if you give this rubric to two people and ask them to evaluate a student, you may get very different results meaning that the rubric is not reliable. The rubric should be like a blueprint and if students follow what it says it is looking for, it will allow them to construct a high quality product.

A better version of this rubric would look like this:

Presentation Rubric

Students: _____   Topic: _____

Overall	Content	Presentation	Visual Aid
Excellent	• Includes many details to make clear the point the student is trying to make. • Has many examples designed to back up what the student is saying. • Research is from reliable sources.	• Speaker presents clearly, does not read to audience. • Speaker makes consistent eye contact with the audience. • Speaker is confident in presentation, is able to answer all questions.	• Uses meaningful visuals that expand the knowledge of what was presented. • Visual aids can be clearly seen by all. • There are several visuals aids from many sources.
Good	• Includes details to make clear the point the student is trying to make in most cases, but a few where it is unclear due to lack of details. • Has some examples to back up points but could use more. • Most of the research is from reliable sources but some questionable or not correct.	• Speaker presents clearly most of the time but every once in a while reads the presentation. • Speaker makes eye contact with the audience by occasionally looks down. • Speaker is confident for most of the presentation, can answer all questions but a couple.	• Uses visuals but not all of them are meaningful, some are just there for decoration rather than expanding of knowledge. • Most visual aids can be seen by all but a few are difficult to make out. • There are a good amount of visuals aids but there are parts where a visual would have been beneficial.
Needs Improvement	• Does not include much detail, making the point the student is trying to make confusing. • Does not use or uses very few examples to back up points. • Much of the research comes from questionable sources or is incorrect.	• Speaker reads the entire presentation or does not make himself clearly heard. • Speaker stares at note cards nearly the entire time, rarely making eye contact with the audience. • Speaker is not confident, has difficult answering most questions	• Lacks visuals or most of them add nothing to the content. • Many of the visuals aids are difficult to see. • There are very few visuals aids or none.

You can see this is more descriptive than the general one from before. There are clear descriptions for what it should look like, which students could follow to prepare their product.

If you would like a brief overall for how to construct an objective rubric that is both reliable and valid, you can watch this Todd Talk https://youtu.be/H_eGyATb4JA. You could also use my Prufrock book, *Using Rubrics for Performance-Based Assessments*, which shows you step-by-step how to create such rubrics.

STEM Design Challenges

Todd Talk Explaining the Strategy
https://youtu.be/F15qtyS4cm4 [3]

Overview of the Strategy

STEM challenges are problem solving that uses the engineering design process in order to be solved:

You first ask students the question that they will seek to answer. It could be something as simple as "How do I build a bridge between these two tables that can support the weight of a baseball?". Part of this might be asking what the constraints of the task are. Constraints can take many forms as follows:

♦ Time
♦ Cost
♦ Materials
♦ Space to work with
♦ Partners

DOI: 10.4324/9781003238577-12

Let's say in the case of this bridge, students are only allowed to use soda straws. Then you allow students to imagine all of the possibilities. This is a brainstorming process where students contribute all the ideas that bubble to the surface no matter how wild. Eventually at the end of this process, students need to have it narrowed down to a single idea they would like to bring to fruition. Once this idea is in place, students begin to plan. This can be informal planning such as talking about what they are going to do, it could be more formal, putting pencil to paper and drawing what they are envisioning. If students skip this step and just begin to create, the results are usually not good. Sometimes it is good to let students find this out for themselves. Sometimes it is something you need to purposefully teach them. After the plan is in place, they can actually create. This is the major lesson that the design process teaches students; that asking, imagining, and planning have to take place before they can just start building and creating. A person building a house does not just eyeball it and nail pieces of wood together randomly. There is a blueprint they are working from. The other lesson students need to learn is that the plan doesn't always work as it was imagined and must be altered. This is why they must experiment with the creating process. If something doesn't seem to be working, change it. If something is lacking, what needs added? This is where the improvement comes in. Is there a way to make this better? What could possibly go wrong that we want to anticipate? Notice that the cycle does not stop there, but rather moves back around to asking. What are new questions we need to ask that have cropped up now that the structure is built?

What It Looks Like in the Classroom

STEM challenges can be long- or short-term. Short-term could be students have an hour to produce their product that solves the problem. Long term means students might be working on it for weeks before showing their final product. Here is an example of a long-term STEM challenge:

You too Can Be a YouTube Star

Essential Questions

- How do you take your interests and make other people interested in it as well?
- How do you explain to someone how to do something so that they understand it?
- How do you make a video that others want to see?

(Continued)

Product

You are going to make a YouTube video that will either be placed on the web for all to see, or you can make it private and show it to a few friends.

The main goal of this video is to teach whoever is watching it how to do what you are showing them. For example, if you are showing them how to cook a dish, do you have all of the steps needed for someone to follow your directions and be able to cook the disk themselves.

You will have the opportunity to share this with the class.

Process

Week 1 – What are you interested in showing others how to do?

Week 2 – What makes a good YouTube video?

Week 3 – How do you teach this interest to someone else in a clear manner?

Weeks 4 and 5 – How to film and edit your YouTube video

Week 6 – Showcase of your own YouTube video

As you can see, this STEM challenge is designed to be 6 weeks long. This would be done with a class as part of the curriculum.

You can have dedicated days where students work on short-term STEM challenges. We would reserve an hour every week on Fridays and designate that as STEM time. This was not part of a class or a curriculum. In fact, we mixed grades together for these STEM times so that they were able to collaborate with students they normally would not get to. We might offer a STEM challenge such as this:

Mini-catapult

Supplies

 ♦ Craft Sticks (Jumbo works better than regular but you can use either size)
 ♦ Rubber bands
 ♦ Plastic bottle cap
 ♦ Glue/Tape
 ♦ Anything they want for ammo (choices will be marshmallows, cotton balls, beans, ping pong balls)

Using the supplies from the list, students must construct a catapult that can launch ammo. They will test their skills at three different stations:

 ♦ Accuracy: A bowl will be in a set location. Teams will have two practice attempts to determine launching distance. Then, from a set distance, students will launch their ammo. Record how many make it into the bowl out of five attempts.

(Continued)

◆ Distance: Set up a launch line using masking tape. Students launch three times per catapult and record each distance using a measuring tape.

◆ Tower: Build a tower out of small plastic cups. Mark a set distance that students must launch behind. See how many of the cups they can knock down in a single launch.

In order to work math into this challenge, you could have an extension that had students

◆ graph distance results for all the catapults in the class;

◆ find the average of the three trials; and

◆ determine how the angle of the launch (how far back they pull the launcher, usually a spoon) affects the distance.

You can have them compete against other groups of students at the various stations.

Where to Find Resources

There are tons of resources online for STEM challenges both long- and short-term. If you simply do a Google search, you get nearly half a million results. Another good place to find short-term STEM challenges are Instant Challenges, which are provided by Destination Imagination. Their task-based challenges usually always use the engineering design process. Here is an example of an instant challenge:

Map Maker

Ask: How do you communicate the directions on a map.

Constraints: You will have up to 5 minutes to create your communication system, up to 2 minutes to communicate the directions, and up to 1 minute to interpret the communication.

◆ 10 Craft Sticks

◆ 20 Toothpicks

◆ 16 Paper Clips

◆ 3 Pieces of Paper

◆ 5 Pieces of String

◆ 2 Styrofoam Cups

◆ 5 Pencils

(Continued)

◆ 1 Marker – The marker may NOT be altered and may NOT be part of your communication system

Materials will be placed on a table in the middle of the room.

Procedure

◆ Part One (5 minutes): Use the materials to create a visual communication system. You should divide your team into communicators and interpreters. Each team member should be in a group and each group must have at least one team member. You will be warned when you have one minute remaining and 30 seconds remaining in Part One.
◆ Part Two (2 minutes): The interpreters should leave the room. The communicators will get a new map with directions. The communicators may place materials on the table. No Team member may talk during Part Two.
◆ Part Three (1 minute): The communicators should leave the room and the interpreters should come back in. The interpreters will get a new blank map and a marker. The interpreters should look at the materials and draw the path from the map with directions onto the blank map. No team member may talk during Part Three.

You could have the team attempt this challenge, reflect on how successful they were, and then try it again to improve.

I also have a series of STEM books available through Prufrock for grades K–1, 2–3, 4–5, and 6–8. Here is an example of one of the challenges from the grades 2–3 book:

Redesigning the Classroom

Big idea: Taking something that you already know and thinking about it in a different way.

Essential question: If you could redesign the classroom, what would you change if anything? What would you add? What would you get rid of?

Constraints

◆ Will use the computer program …
◆ Must be able to fit in 30 students and a teacher
◆ Have to be realistic about choices
◆ Cannot alter the physical space of the room any (i.e., adding windows, taking out walls)

Deliverables: Students will design the classroom either in a 2D drawing or a 3D model. This model should represent the dimensions of the actual classroom.

Suggested Timeline

Day 1 Determine the size and layout of the current classroom *Ask*	Day 2 Imagine what you could add to the classroom to make it better *Imagine*	Day 3 Plan what your design might look like *Plan*	Day 4 Decide how you are going to create your design *Plan*	Day 5 Begin to create your design *Create*
Day 6 Continue to create your design *Create*	Day 7 Continue to create your design *Create*	Day 8 Improve any aspects of the design based on suggestions *Improve*	Day 9 Present your version of the redesigned classroom	Day 10 Discussion over the best suggestions for the classroom *Improve*

In this STEM challenge, you can see the math involved where students must determine the measurements of the room. You could even challenge them further by having them calculate the perimeter and volume. Engineering is represented by the design of the room with its new furniture and layout. The technology comes in the fact that students must find a computer program where they can represent the ideas they have in mind for the room. You will also notice that the calendar even lays out the steps to the engineering design process.

If you want to create your own STEM challenges, keep in mind, they do not have to all have science, technology, engineering, and math. As long as you have two of them and students use the engineering design process, then that qualifies as a STEM challenge. Here is a STEM challenge matrix that might help you generate ideas:

Materials	Construct	Purpose
Cotton balls	Radio/television	Signal aliens
Aluminum foil	Monument	Make life easier
Mailing labels	Game/Sport	Communicate
Paper plates/cups	Bridge	Safety/Protection
Cardboard	Tool	Hit a target
Toilet paper/paper towel rolls	Container	Moves
Spaghetti	Shelter	Support weight
Play-Doh	Vehicle	Reach a goal
Construction paper	Product	Signals
Plastic straws	Musical instrument	Brings people together

You would take a material or materials from the first column, and construct something with it that serves a purpose from the third column.

What Impact It Will Have on Your Teaching/ Classroom

Depending on how you decide to offer these STEM challenges, it will have an impact on your daily class time. These STEM challenges are not something students begin independently. It would be introduced to the class by the teacher and then worked on however long they have been given. It would consume the class during this work time. If you have reserved an hour on a Friday for STEM time, that class time will be impacted. If you decide to do it as part of a multi-week unit, that will be the focus of your class for that duration. You could always find a way to link it to a content standard and that way the STEM challenge actually becomes a part of your curriculum. I was responsible for the following standard in my science class:

Revise an existing design used to solve a problem

I had students redesigning the mousetrap, only their constraint was that the trap could not harm the mouse as the original one does:

Invent a Better Mousetrap and the World Will Beat a Path to Your Door

Description
The aforementioned saying refers to the fact that if you improve upon an already-existing product, you will become successful. Technology must always change to meet the needs of people. Could you imagine if we had never changed the original computer which was so large it took up an entire room? We are going to revisit a classic design of a product and try to improve upon it.

You will create a new mousetrap, one that captures the mouse without doing it harm unlike the original model. You will design the mousetrap first and then build a working model that will capture a stuffed mouse. Your design must include steps by step how to create it, measurements, materials, and be detailed enough that if someone were to build the mousetrap using the design, they would be able to do so. You will also need to compare and contrast your mousetrap with the original one and evaluate which is better and why.

(Continued)

Suggested Materials
   Graph paper/drawing paper
   Materials to build mousetrap

Timeline of Project

- ◆ Introduction to Project/Review of old design – 1 day
- ◆ Design of trap – 2 days
- ◆ Construction of model – 3 days
- ◆ Comparison of the two mousetraps – 2 days
- ◆ Presentation/Demonstration – 1 day

Products

- ◆ Design of your mousetrap
- ◆ Model of your mousetrap and demonstration of it
- ◆ Comparison between your mousetrap and the original

How Much Work It Will Require of You to Successfully Execute It

One of the biggest issues with STEM challenges is finding the supplies needed for students to work with. If you are asking them to use toilet paper rolls, then you have to have enough of them for all of the groups working on the challenge. This can be costly depending on what materials are needed for the challenge. For the egg drop challenge I do with students, it requires them to have tube socks and plastic straws as some of their materials. That means I have to trudge over to the store and buy a package of tube socks and a set of straws. There are other materials I need for the challenge that I can just get for free such as plastic grocery bags, golf balls from my golf bag, and paper from the supply closet. For the cardboard, I can ask the custodians to set aside some boxes from the lunchroom.

It is best to find challenges that work within your budget, or if you have a supply of materials (we always had bins full of various STEM supplies for our Friday challenge hour), we would choose a task that used these materials or substitute something we did have for something we did not. You can always ask students to bring in empty tissue boxes, paper towel rolls, cardboard boxes, and other such materials to build up your STEM collection.

Creative Thinking

Todd Talk Explaining the Strategy
https://youtu.be/Obb6xsBVv3U [3]

Overview of the Strategy

When asked to imagine a creative thinker, oftentimes we think of students who have a lot of artistic creativity. These two things can be the same but they can also be different. Someone who shows a lot of creativity might display this in paintings, music, poetry, and other such creative outlets. Creative thinkers are those students who think outside the box. We use that term a lot, but what does it really mean? What it can look like is when you ask a classroom full of students an open-ended question, a majority of the class gives the most obvious, surface-level answer. A creative thinker gets underneath it all and looks a little deeper, seeing something that others have not. This is what outside the box thinking looks like.

For example, I once had a group of students participating in Destination Imagination, a creative thinking competition. They were taking part in the instant challenge and were given a large bottle of water, a dozen nails, and a couple of pieces of paper. Their task was to try and fit as many of the nails as possible on top of the bottle of water. The time began and the group began discussing possibilities, all of a sudden one of the students reached over and turned the bottle of water upside down so that the cap was on the ground and the bigger bottom surface was at the top now. With this increased surface area, they were easily able to get all 12 nails on it. When I spoke to the judges later, they told me that they saw lots of possible solutions, but all of them were using the bottle of water like it typically lay. My group was the only one who thought to turn it upside down (and the only one who got all 12 nails on top). Not even the judges had considered it.

There are differences between gifted learners, bright or high achievers, and creative thinkers. Bertie Kingore (2003) compiled a list to show these:

Gifted	Bright	Creative
Works independently	Enjoys working in groups	Likes to do it "their way"
Sometimes is not focused	Follows directions	Very alert
Creates abstract humor	Understands abstract humor	Off-the-wall humor

(Continued)

DOI: 10.4324/9781003238577-13

Gifted	Bright	Creative
Guesses and infers well	Good memorizers	Brainstorms well
Is curious	Is interested	Wonders
Manipulates information	Absorbs information	Improvises
Poses new questions	Remembers the answer	Sees exceptions
Already knows	Learns easily	Asks "what if"
Is selectively interested	Is attentive	Daydreams
Generates complex ideas	Generates advanced ideas	Has lots of ideas but may never develop
Is self-critical	Is pleased with own learning	Never finished with possibilities
Is constantly developing	Is accurate	Is original
Answers with depth	Answers with detail	Injects new possibilities
Needs 1–2 repetitions to master	Needs 6–8 repetitions to master	Questions the need for mastery
Prefers peer-mates	Prefers age-mates	Prefers creative peers or work by self

As you can see, there are some distinct differences between these three learners. In schools, we offer lots of classes that meet the needs of the high achiever, some schools offer specific classes to meet the needs of gifted students, but very rarely are educators focused on the way creative thinkers learn. This is why it is important to be purposeful about teaching creative thinking in your classroom.

What It Looks Like in the Classroom

You do not have to have lessons that solely teach creative thinking. Instead, you should take your already-existing lessons and do a few things to bring out the creative thinker in these students. It is about creating a culture of creative thinking.

The first of these is to encourage students to take risks. We often tell students that it is OK to fail, and then turn around andgive them a poor grade, in essence punishing them for taking a risk. Instead we need to show students that making a mistake is perfectly fine, especially if you are able to learn from it. Your philosophy should be:

F – FIRST
A – ATTEMPT
I – IN
L – LEARNING

What this means is you should create a culture in your classroom where it is not only alright to make a mistake, but also it is highly encouraged if it means you are trying something outside of your comfort zone. After all, this is where the greatest learning takes place.

One such activity I have seen a teacher do with students is what she called "my favorite mistake". Students would look over their math homework and determine if they had made any errors. If they did, they had to explain the error and how they learned from it:

My Favorite Mistake		
Name: _____ Date: _____ Class:_____		
Assignment: _____ Problem: _____		
Original Work	**What was the mistake?**	**Correct Work**
Why was this your favotite mistake?	**What did you learn from this mistake?**	

By encouraging students that it is fine to make mistakes means that they will use their creative thinking, and yes, sometimes they will bite off more than they can chew, but again, this is where they are going to learn the most. I would much rather have a student who made a mistake and learned something meaningful from it than one who successfully did a simple task but gained no enduring understanding.

The second thing you could do in your classroom is to ask open-ended questions or have open-ended problems. Open-ended questions are those without a correct answer. Examples of open-ended questions would be:

Science: Is there life on other planets?
    ELA: How would the story have been different if Harry Potter were not an orphan?
    Social Studies: Is our president a good one??
    Math: The answer is 37. What is the question?

Students must use creative thinking to come up with a unique, but plausible solution. It can also be accomplished by using such inquiry strategies like problem-based learning. Problem-based learning often asks students to attempt to solve big hairy problems. These are problems without an easy solution where students must be creative with their ideas. An example would be how do we stop global warming? Allow students to research all sorts of solutions as well as creating their own, and then present the one that they feel will be most successful.

In addition to asking your questions, you must give them space to create and to ask their own questions. Part of their creative thinking is driven by their curiosity. Give them space to explore these questions. Socratic seminars are an excellent way for students to use questioning skills to learn about something. Here are some general guidelines for students in a Socratic Seminar:

1. Be prepared to participate and ask good questions.
2. Show respect for differing ideas, thoughts, and values
3. Allow each speaker enough time to begin and finish his or her thoughts
4. Involve others in the discussion, ask them to elaborate on their responses
5. Build on what others say: ask questions to probe deeper, clarify, and add
6. Participate openly and keep your mind open to new ideas and possibilities.
7. Give evidence and examples to support your response.
8. Discuss the ideas, not each other's opinions or personal experiences.

When considering classroom activities, determine whether they use convergent or divergent thinking. Here are the major differences between convergent and divergent thinking:

Convergent	Divergent
Logical	Inquiry
Objective	Subjective
Intellectual	Emotional
Realistic	Imaginative
Planned	Impulsive
Systematic	Holistic
Structured	By the seat of pants
Quantitative	Qualitative

You can see that the divergent thinking is right along the lines of your creative thinker. But you can also see the importance of the convergent thinking when it comes to learning. A balance of the two would be ideal. You can have a set of math problems that use logic to solve, but then follow that up with a reflection where students share their feelings about the learning. If you are using inquiry learning, you still have to have a structure to keep students focused. Students can use their imagination to solve realistic, world problems. Being aware of the yin and yang of these two types of thinking will help you to better address the needs of your creative thinkers.

A final strategy you might consider to foster creative thinking is to incorporate art into your core content areas. This allows students to see how art and the real world work together. An example would be using the painting "The Nighthawks" by Edward Hopper and asking students to write a story based on the scene. Or looking at the geometric shapes that Picasso uses in his art. Or using the carving of the Boston Massacre by Paul Revere to have a discussion about propaganda and the way the British were portrayed as compared to actual reported events.

There are many other strategies you can use in a classroom with creative thinkers. The most important thing is to have activities that give them the chance to be creative. Close-ended, factual only, producing something the teacher provides are ways to stifle this creative thinking.

Where to Find Resources

An excellent resource would be the Creativity and Education website https:// creativityandeducation.com/. On this, there are tons of resources for how to teach creativity in the classroom. In addition, they host a YouTube channel called CreateTUBity which had videos on creative thinking challenges, a creative thinking course for students, and creativity for teachers. It can be accessed at https://www.youtube.com/channel/UCDvd6niIwmsf1Lce8V8jfXg.

What Impact It Will Have on Your Teaching/ Classroom

Deliberately teaching creative thinking would be a 3 in that it might not change the way you teach, but it will hopefully cause you to be more cognizant of these types of thinkers in your classroom and provide activities to challenge them. It is about creating a culture in your class where creative thinking is both encouraged and expected. It is also about you, the teacher, developing an awareness for such a student. When that student gives a seemingly off-the-wall response to a simple answer, explore that a little bit, try to get to what the student is thinking. You might be surprised to find out how much thought went into it.

How Much Work It Will Require of You to Successfully Execute It

Part of this is teaching students the skills needed to be a creative thinker. It is not enough to have a good idea, you want to have the skills to make a good idea happen. There are five skills you can teach that will help students with this:

◆ Imagination: Have activities where you are asking students to imagine. This could be in ELA class where you ask students to image how a book they have been reading might end. It could be in social studies where you ask students to imagine how things would have been different if history had gone another way (i.e. what if the Japanese had not invaded Pearl Harbor). In science, it could be imagining a hypothesis for an experiment, trying to predict all of the possible outcomes and determining which one makes the most sense. Even in math you can ask students to imagine another method for solving a problem.

◆ Organization: What learning this skill does is allows students to take their many unique ideas and boil it down to something usable. Part of this is time management, prioritization, and initiative. These are all skills that can be taught to students. Without this discipline, their ideas never take any sort of shape and so they do not get to bring their imagination to fruition.

◆ Grit: This is the ability to continue going forward after experiencing an obstacle or setback. Some gifted students have not developed grit because things have always come so easy to them. This becomes a problem once they are challenged. Teaching students strategies for how to overcome difficulty or what it looks like to adapt when something does not go as planned.

◆ Collaboration: This is the ability to work with others, a skill that any place of business would covet in a potential employee. We often throw students into a group and hope for the best. What if instead, you taught students what success collaboration looks like. This would include establishing norms as to group expectations, learning how to troubleshoot when problems arise, and figuring out how to best utilize the strengths to the betterment of the final product, synergizing all of the creativity in the group.

◆ Responsibility: Have them develop their own projects where they create the learning objectives, determine the product, map out their timeline, and gather their own resources. An easy way to start this with students is by giving them more choice in the classroom. This choice then gives them responsibility for their own learning including where they can take their imagination and what they can create with it.

These skills can be woven into work so they do not need to be lessons on their own, but they do need to be deliberately taught. To just expect these things to happen without guidance is not going to help the creative thinker in using their abilities to the utmost.

Depth and Complexity

Todd Talk Explaining the Strategy
https://youtu.be/R-zxPbR1RXw [3]

Overview of the Strategy

Depth and Complexity is a thinking platform that was developed by Dr. Sandra Kaplan, Bette Gould, and Sheila Madsen for the California State Department in 1994. It was devised as a way to get children to take what they were learning deeper. It started first with the concepts, which then became icons in order to help students learn them better. This allowed a teacher to just place the icon on a piece of work the student was assigned and the student would know to use that concept to dig down into the work. It was a way to differentiate for gifted students. Its creation came from four sources:

1. A review of Advanced Placement curriculum and assessment
2. A study of California Golden State Exam requirements
3. Conventional wisdom about the nature of academic disciplines
4. A review of classic literature

This is especially good with gifted students because it challenges them, encourages them to make connections, allows for tiered assignments depending on how deep a student can go, and makes them the expert.

What It Looks Like in the Classroom

Depth and Complexity has 11 icons that are used to elicit deeper thinking in students. Eight of these are for depth, three are for complexity. The icons look like this:

DOI: 10.4324/9781003238577-14

 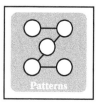 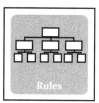 

Icon	Definition
Language of the Discipline	Vocabulary terms specific to the content or discipline.
Details	Examples and evidence to support opinions and ideas.
Ethics	The moral principles involved including controversy and arguments.
Unanswered Questions	This is what is not yet clear. What still needs to be addressed or what is missing?
Over Time	The relation of something in the past, present, and future. What changes and why do they do so?
Across Disciplines	How the concept is seen in other subject areas.
Trends	Factors that cause events to occur.
Patterns	When someone reoccurs, what is its sequence, can you predict what will happen next?
Big Ideas	A general statement that applies to ideas, and what is the main one.
Rules	The guidelines and regulations that provide structure.
Multiple Perspectives	An event seen through several different sets of eyes.

The icons act as visual thinking tools. The students see these and it challenges them to go beyond the basics (depth). It also asks them to think more critically about the topic (complexity). Eight of these icons are used to get depth:

An example would be in math class where the teacher is going over angles. The teacher puts this icon on the assignment.

Students must then brainstorm all of the possible terms that might be used with angles:

Acute	Transversal	Obtuse
Inscribed	Central	Straight
Alternate exterior	Interior	Adjoining
Complimentary	Supplementary	Alternate interior
Right	Corresponding	Exterior

Not only that, students have to understand how to use the terms and to identify these angles when they see them. The language of the discipline icon has pushed their thinking to consider what specific terms are used for the various angles so that when the teacher uses this language, they will know what it means.

These three icons aim at complexity:

An example would be in your history class wherein you are teaching students about the Civil War. You write this topic on the board and either use your icon magnet or you draw the icon yourself.

Students then shout out the obvious:

North

South

The teacher patiently waits, knowing students can dig deeper, eyeballing the icon. Suddenly, a student says:

Slaves

Another one chimes in:

Farmers

And pretty soon you have compiled a list of different perspectives of the Civil War:

Women

Farmers

Soldiers

Plantation owners

Politicians

Native Americans

You can use this list to have a debate, a discussion, write a journal entry in someone else's shoes, or many other products that would allow these perspectives to be explored.

In addition to using the icons by themselves, they can be combined. To help students to know when to use the proper icon and to channel their thinking, you could use a graphic organizer such as this:

Grade:		Begin Date:	
Unit:		End Date:	

🏛 **Domain:**

🏛 ❄ **Standard(s):**

❄ **Objective: I will...**

👄 **Language and Key Academic Vocabulary:**

👓 **Prior Knowledge and Common Misconceptions:**

Students are encouraged to uncover the big idea of the unit. They will unpack the standard and see what its details are and its main idea. As they begin to shake out the learning objective, they must pay attention to the details so that something is not overlooked. It is also important for students to know the language and key vocabulary of what they are learning. Finally, they will consider this topic from multiple perspectives and surmise common misconceptions. Students can take their thoughts about each of these and use the icons to remind them to go deeper.

Another graphic organizer that is effective with the icons would be framing:

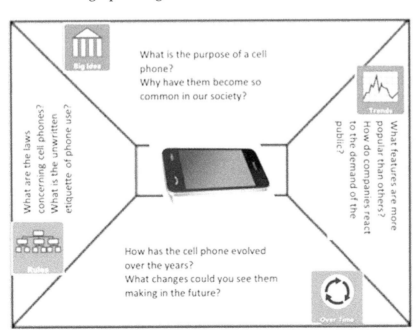

This is simply a graphic organizer that allows you to organize the icons and to provoke the thinking you are seeking in your students. Each and every question here could be discussed and debated at length or written about by students. Something such as this would certainly give a student a lot to think about.

Where to Find Resources

The best place to look for resources would be with J. Taylor Education who holds the copyright to the icons. You could certainly use Depth and Complexity without the official icons, but they have products such as posters you can place around the room to create the proper culture in your classroom, magnetic icons you can throw on the whiteboard to remind students which icon the lesson is focusing on, and there are sets of Q3 cards that can be used to help teachers construct questions centered around the various icons. In addition, they have differentiation software that a district can get a year-long license for. The software allows you to create differentiation task statements for three different levels of learners.

What Impact It Will Have on Your Teaching/ Classroom

This would be a 3 because in reality, you can keep doing the same lessons you have always done. You just need to determine when there are opportunities to use one of the icons to get students to go a little deeper. By adding icons to your daily assignments, to your discussions, to your projects, and to your assessments, can raise the rigor in your classroom and have them engage in the thinking that these icons are asking for.

This will also help you with differentiation. Whereas before a lesson only had a cursory understanding, using an icon to bolster the thinking can take it to the next level. Let us take this lesson on the book *Night* by Elie Wiesel. It is an autobiography about a teenage boy and his life spent in the concentration camps during World War II.

If you were to use this icon:

There would be tons of questions to consider about the book. Questions such as follows:

♦ Should you stick up for people being mistreated if it means you will be punished as well?
♦ How strong is family?
♦ Is there evil in the world?
♦ Is it every man/woman for him/herself?
♦ What is permitted in war?
♦ Should the young remain innocent?
♦ Should you always obey your government?
♦ Is being a camp guard just a job or should people take what they are doing into consideration?

There are many more that you could provide or have students come up with on their own. You could also use this icon:

How much history is contained in *Night*? What can we learn about the past to prevent the future? This could be combined with this icon:

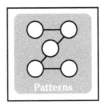

You could have students look for patterns where history repeats itself? Why does genocide keep happening and how can we prevent it in the future? These icons will certainly cause your students to think much deeper.

How Much Work It Will Require of You to Successfully Execute It

Most of the work for Depth and Complexity comes in teaching students what the various icons mean and how this should jumpstart their thinking. You can do this at the very beginning of the year, having an introductory unit that explains each of the icons and shows students how they can be used. You can ask students to create a frame about themselves in which they choose four icons to describing themselves:

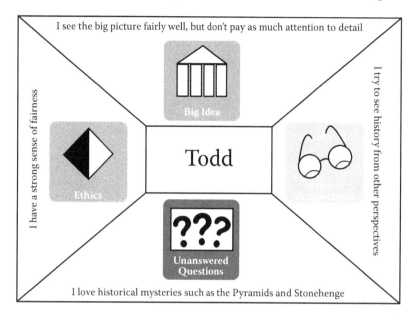

This is also a good lesson to get to know more about your students.

The more familiar students become with the icons, the more they will be able to use them. They will get to the point where they will know what icon to use before you even suggest it.

Student Choice/Choice Boards

Todd Talk Explaining the Strategy
https://youtu.be/lpDCeC3bCkU
https://youtu.be/Uj3T8vTVixY [4]

Overview of the Strategy

Student choice is not just letting students do whatever they want. Student choice is allowing students to make choices within a learning structure. It does not mean there are not times where students cannot go outside of this structure, or box so to speak. The structure is there much as a frame of a house is there. You can build on anything you want to it, but the frame is there underneath to hold it all together and keep it from collapsing.

These choices may be in the manner and method they will be learning about something, whether it be the topic, the method for learning about it, or the product. This can also include the level of challenge they are willing to take on as well as what questions need to be asked. It can even be innocuous choices such as where they sit in the classroom, who they work with, or when the product will be due. By allowing students this choice, it makes them a part of the learning process where they feel like they have some control over their education and as a result, are more invested and willing to put forth effort because of this buy-in.

There are many places where you can use student choice in the classroom:

Easy Choices	More Difficult Choices
Seating	Product
Music	Assessment
Group members	Questions
Audience	Homework
Resources	Self-evaluation
Due date	Content
Topic	Time management
Help	Challenge

DOI: 10.4324/9781003238577-15

You can start with the easy ones at first if you are uncomfortable with students having such control, and the more comfortable you get, the more willing you will be to give over other more important aspects of the classroom.

One thing to help students with their choices is to provide choice boards. A choice board, also sometimes called a menu board, is a guided choice, where you provide students with several options, which they get to decide. Here is an example of a menu board designed to push students to a greater depth of understanding:

Menu Board

Choose an Appetizer

Remember details about the lesson.
    Demonstrate *understanding* of the lesson.

Choose a Side Dish

Apply the lesson to something in your own life.
    Analyze the lesson and decide what information is most important to you

Choose a Main Dish

Create a product that demonstrates mastery of the lesson.
    Evaluate the importance of the lesson to you.

Choose a Dessert

Provide a *reflection* on something you learned from the lesson that you hadn't expected to?

Notice that this menu board differentiates by starting out with lower-level thinking tasks such as remembering and understanding. Then students must take it a step further and apply what they have learned to an authentic situation, as well as analyzing what the most important lessons would be. For the end of the lesson, we scaffold students up to the highest levels of thinking, allowing them to create a product that demonstrates their mastery of the learning, as well as evaluating the importance of the lesson. It all closes with a reflection in which students ask themselves what they learned that was a surprise for them. This is that a-ha moment where you truly gain an understanding of what students got from the lesson and whether it was meaningful to them. For each step the student takes through the lesson, the more challenging the thinking becomes. In this type of menu board, the students are choosing how they will demonstrate, apply, create, and reflect.

Another way you can offer student choice is through the activities or product that they produce. Here is a general choice board for ELA known as the Tic Tac Toe:

Tic Tac Toe Choice Board

Complete a row of three squares

Change the setting of the novel. Describe how this setting would change the story and why.	What do you think about the motives of at least three of the main characters? Why do you think they drive these people?	Choose a passage and find ten words you do not know that you think are important to what is being discussed in the passage. Making a glossary so that others can reference it or create flashcards for them.
Write a diary entry or draw a picture of a scene from the perspective of one of the minor characters. How might they see what is going on in the book differently than others?	Student choice	Write a song for the novel that captures its main theme. You can choose to perform this or not.
Present a monologue, create a PowerPoint, or make a WeVideo from the perspective of one of the characters and how they view the protagonist and the antagonist.	With a partner answer the following questions: 1. Who is the main character of the story? 2. What is the problem in the story? 3. What is the setting of your story?	Replace characters in the book with members of a popular television show or movie. How would these characters act in the story and would it change things?

Students would then have to complete three of the activities either using the book the class is reading collectively, or if this is independent reading choice, using their book. Notice the center square also provides students with the choice of creating their own activity/product. The choice board is a mixture of lower-level and higher-level activities, so if the student does three of them, he or she might get one that is lower level but he or she will also have to expand his or her thinking by completing a higher level one as well.

What It Looks Like in the Classroom

Choice boards can be fairly complex but you can certainly keep things simple. This was the choice board I offered in my science classes:

Product Choices

1. Demonstration
2. Electronic portfolio
3. Essay
4. Exhibition
5. Journal
6. Research paper
7. Presentation
8. Portfolio
9. Performance
10. Test

Students could choose one of these ten as their product to demonstrate mastery of learning the content standards. This choice allowed students to select products that they felt comfortable with or if they wanted to challenged themselves, they could choose something that would develop a skill. For example, if the student was a strong writer but not a great speaker, she might choose the essay, journal, or research paper option. However, if another student hates to write and yet explains himself well, he could do an exhibition or the presentation. If a third student had never created a portfolio before but wanted to give it a try, I would provide exemplars for them to see what the product looked like. One thing you need to be sure of is to show students what each of these looks like. I had a pretty specific format for the electronic portfolio that I wanted students to follow. I wanted to define what a performance was and was not. The test option actually refers to the student making a test for others to take, not taking one themselves. They were required to provide an answer key as well. I spent an entire class going over what each of these looked like. I also saved work from previous years to show students what the finished product might look like. Students would then indicate to me which product they were going to produce so that I could coach them in a proper manner when we sat down to have conferences.

You can be more specific with students what activities they need to accomplish to demonstrate mastery. This math choice board has very specific tasks for students to do, but they can determine which of the two they would like to do:

Choice Board Math

M (Mastery)	A (Application)	T (Taking It to the Next Level)	H (Honing Your Skills)
Be able to explain the rules for adding decimals	Complete problems 1–5 concerning decimals.	Come up with 10 problems of your own that use the rules of decimals (provide an answer key as well)	Create a game where participants must use decimals in order to play
Watch the Khan Academy video on decimals and summarize what you learned from it	Be able to use decimals when dealing with money in a real-life situation	Take a look at the sample problem and try to find where a mistake was made, correcting it	You are given $172.82. Buy yourself a back-to-school wardrobe

Notice these scaffold as they go along. When you start with the first activity, you are simply showing a basic understanding. You then take the next step of applying what was learned to show you know how to use it. Then you are taking it to the next level, expanding the learning as is necessary for gifted students. The final activities have to do with creating, taking the concept and putting it into a real-world situation. By students going through this, it should be enriching their learning.

Finally, what do you do with that student who finishes his work early and seems to have nothing to do? How can you guide him to dig deeper into what he learned? You could use a choice board such as this:

Enrichment Activities for Those Who Finish Early

Dig: Can you go deeper into what you just learned?	Project: How could you turn this lesson into a project?	Master: Determine whether you have mastered the concept or just finished it
Partner: If someone else finishes early trade work and critique one another	Trouble-shoot: Ask students to list problems with the lesson and how to fix it	Plan: Ask students to plan an extension lesson
Extend: How could you create the next level of the lesson to further teach the concept	Reflect: How could you make your work even better? What are things that you could improve?	Refresh: Take a quick nap to refresh your brain for the next lesson

These are all asking students to push themselves and their understanding of what they learned, and dig a little deeper.

Where to Find Resources

You can find all sorts of examples of choice board online. I have several examples of choice boards shared here and others which can be found at www.thegiftedguy.com/resources under the heading of Resources to Fill Your Gifted Toolbox. I also have a colleague Stephanie Howell who is excellent at making choice boards which she generously shares through her Twitter account @mrshowell24.

   If you really want to offer students more choice, have them come up with the choices, generating a menu board with their own ideas. You could brainstorm ideas as a class, or have them write ideas on sticky notes and then place them on the whiteboard.

What Impact It Will Have on Your Teaching/ Classroom

Using the strategy will have a fairly big impact on your classroom. The students are going to be the ones steering the boat. The decisions they make will have an effect on the feedback you provide, the way you assess mastery, the materials you need to have available, your classroom calendar, and your day-to-day operations. Because you can mix and match lesser choices in the classroom, this is not a 5, but it can be depending on the level of choice you allow your students to have. There are some choices that will have minor effects on your classroom such as seating, music being played, partners for groups, and whether they want your help or not.

   Know that the more choice you give to your students, the more your teaching will be affected, but also know that this affect can be a good thing and provides your students with the confidence to become self-motivated individuals who show initiative instead of waiting for the teacher to tell them what they need to do.

How Much Work It Will Require of You to Successfully Execute It

Giving over control to students to make choices usually reserved for the teacher can be a tough thing to do. Especially with the need to teach the content standards within a given time, some teachers feel as though they have to run a tight ship in order to get through all of the material.

I can tell you from personal experience though that once you start to give students choice, you will see motivation improve because students have a say-so in their education and are being treated as a partner in the learning. Quite frankly, giving your students more choice means you have to do less work and planning. If they decide a particular product to demonstrate mastery, it will be up to them to learn how to create it. Rather than you finding resources for students to read about a topic, they search the internet independently and find the information that will be helpful to them.

The major aspect of giving students the choice to do things is being alright with the choices that they make. A student may make a choice that you know is going to put her way over her head, but she might surprise you and pull it off. Even if he or she does not, he or she will hopefully learn from this mistake and make better choices the next time. Or if two students notorious for goofing off and distracting one another decide to work together in a group, being content with this decision and allowing them to learn the tough lesson iof not always picking your best bud if you are expecting quality work.

Students as Teachers

Todd Talk Explaining the Strategy
https://youtu.be/B7g05ALPMic [4]

Overview of the Strategy

Simply put, sometimes our students know more than we do. They are passionate about something and thus have learned more about it and there isn't much you can introduce to them that they do not already know. When you have these so-called experts in your class, why not let them teach the lesson? I had a fifth grader named John. He loved outer space. Watched the Nova channel all the time, read books dealing with it, and studied everything he could get his hands on. Low and behold, one of the fifth grade units was on space. I knew within about five minutes of talking with John at the beginning of the school year that he was very passionate about space. Knowing this, I asked him a question before we began the unit.

"How comfortable would you be teaching us something about space"?

"Pretty comfortable", he said in his youthful confidence.

"I will give you one of our 45-minutes periods to teach myself and the class anything about space that you want to".

"I can teach about blackholes"?

"Yes, that would be great. It does require that you create a lesson plan though that I need to look over. You also want to consider how you are going to teach us either through lecture, hands-on, a project, or something else".

"I think I can do that".

"You have two weeks to develop this plan and then I'll have you teach us on Friday, the 15th".

"I'm teaching the entire class"?

"Yes. Do you think you can do that"?

"I do", and he got to work.

As I went through the space unit with the other students, John would be at the back of the room at one of the computers, researching anything he could find on blackholes. When I would get the class working on something in groups, I would walk over and informally check-in with John, but most times I just seemed to be in his way. He had a couple of formal checks where I would look over his lesson plan, offer him advice, and make sure he had

DOI: 10.4324/9781003238577-16

everything he needed. On that Friday, I turned the class over to John. He spend the entire 45 minutes (I actually had to stop him) teaching the class what he knew and had learned about blackholes, showing pictures that had been taken of them and explaining research that had been done on them. It wasn't the greatest lesson, but John was able to share his knowledge with the class in a productive manner, and the class was able to learn from him.

What It Looks Like in the Classroom

You are not always going to have a John in your classroom, but students are very capable of learning about something and teaching it to the class. Keep in mind, this is way different from tutoring, which I said earlier was a bad thing to have gifted students do. In that case, the gifted student is having to slow himself or herself down and not work at the same level of understanding because of the student's struggles. Teaching the class on the other hand is being on the same level as your peers if not higher, trying to explain something at the level they are capable of.

In addition, by teaching the class, the chances of retention are much higher than other methods of learning:

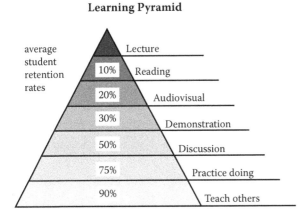

Learning Pyramid

average student retention rates

	Lecture
10%	Reading
20%	Audiovisual
30%	Demonstration
50%	Discussion
75%	Practice doing
90%	Teach others

Think about it, the student has to have a very good understanding in order to teach it to someone else. And this understanding many times has to be more than just the surface level because if it is not clear to some or they have a question, the student needs to be able to address this.

I have done this is various ways in my classroom. One method was when I had a unit with six sections to it, I put students in groups of five with each one responsible for a section. They had to teach and assess it, meaning they had to have some method of checking that others gained mastery of what was taught. They were given an allotment of time, usually half an hour, and could use any teaching method they wanted. This had two motives behind it. First, I could cover a lot of ground doing it this way. Instead of taking 6 weeks to cover those sections, I could give students two weeks to prepare and give the lesson. Second, it caused students to have a much greater appreciation of teaching and how difficult a task it is. It would crack me up because my students often complained I used PowerPoint too much, and yet when I allowed them to choose any method of teaching the material they wanted, five of the six groups did use a PowerPoint.

Another way that I did the student as a teacher was to divide a large topic into much smaller subtopics. For example, when we learned about Egypt, I let students choose topics that were of interest to them from prior knowledge or information we had covered. I would get 20 requests for the pyramids or a dozen for mummification, but I would also get some interesting ones such as the Nile, the jobs they held, the clothes they wore, Hieroglyphics, and others. I let these groups form organically based on student interest, with one group having eight students while another one might be a single person. The student(s) would become an expert on this topic and teach it to the rest of the class. I felt this allowed students to learn in-depth about one thing rather than get the very basics of a bunch of them. In addition, it allowed them to learn many 21st-century skills, including accessing and analyzing information, effective oral and written communication, critical thinking, adaptability, and collaboration if they were working with others.

A third way you could organize it would be to take a specific lesson and divide it into chunks for better understanding, making student groups responsible for each chunk. One of my favorite projects I did with students was the Schoolhouse Rocks one. I took the US Constitution and broke it up into chunks, asking student groups to write and give a performance set to the tune of a famous song that would teach others the basic concepts. Groups were also responsible for creating quizzes to make sure the other students got it. Even though it was nearly 20 years ago, I'll never forget the group who while teaching up about how laws were made, set their song to the tune of "Who Let the Dogs Out". They changed the chorus of "Who let the dogs out, who, who, who" to the humorous but appropriate "Who made the nation's laws, rich, white, guys".

Then there were those rarer situations where I had a student such as John who possessed a passion for a subject, an experience, or a skill that I did not and I wanted to tap into that resource. When I had a unit on immigration, I asked foreign exchange students to come in and talk to the class about their experiences. I had a student who had taken a vacation to the Mayan temples in Mexico and she had taken a lot of photos, she was given time to share what she had seen and experienced. If I saw a student who understood a math concept in much depth while others were just trying to gain a basic understanding, I would ask this student to demonstrate problems and explain how he was solving them on the board.

Where to Find Resources

Your students are the resources in this case. The only things you need to provide are internet access and depending on their age, maybe some guiding websites to get them started which might look like this:

Resources for Power

- ◆ Identify various forms of natural resources and how we harness them for their power.
  - • A place you might get started:
    - • http://www.energy.gov/energysources/index.htm
- ◆ Explain how the supply of many non-renewable resources for power is limited and can be extended through reducing, reusing and recycling but cannot be extended indefinitely.
  - • A place you might get started:
    - • http://www.eia.doe.gov/kids/energy.cfm?page=nonrenewable_home-basics
- ◆ Investigate ways Earth's renewable resources for power (e.g. freshwater, air) can be maintained.
  - • A place you might get started:
    - • http://www.windows2universe.org/earth/Water/water_cycle.html
- ◆ Investigate positive and negative impacts of human activity and technology on the environment when it comes to natural resources and power.
  - • A place you might get started:
    - • https://www.energy.gov/eere/wind/environmental-impacts-and-siting-wind-projects

The important thing for this type of enrichment is to teach students how to properly research. Knowing that students will be doing a lot of independent research in my class, I spend a few days at the beginning of the year training students on how to conduct internet research. Here is a basic lesson plan of what I work with my students on:

Step 1: Formulate Research Questions

Start by writing specific research questions. Doing so will help you narrow your topic and determine exactly what information you need.

Sample questions:

- ◆ How do volcanoes form?
- ◆ What causes volcanoes to erupt?
- ◆ Can we predict volcanic eruptions?

Step 2: List Possible Sources of Information

Before going online, try to identify any sources that might have information on your topic. For example, you might list:

(Continued)

- ◆ government agencies, such as FEMA (Federal Emergency Management Agency), or the National Park Service;
- ◆ museums with exhibits on volcanoes;
- ◆ university science departments specializing in volcano research; or
- ◆ *National Geographic* or PBS/NOVA might have TV documentaries on famous volcanoes or volcanic eruptions. Perhaps they would also have information or interactive explorations on their Web sites.

Step 3: Identify Keywords

Review the questions and sources you brainstormed in steps 1–2, and circle the keywords. Your list of keywords might look something like the following:

Table 16.1

Keywords	
Terms	**Possible Sources**
◆ Volcanoes ◆ Volcanologists ◆ Erupt/eruptions ◆ Form ◆ Active volcanoes ◆ Famous volcanoes	◆ FEMA ◆ National Park Service ◆ Museums ◆ *National Geographic* ◆ PBS or NOVA

Step 4: Ready... Set... Search

You're finally ready to choose a tool(s) and begin your search. Depending on the time you have and your own personal preference, you can start with a search engine, directory, or a specific site of your own choice. Here are three possible ways you might begin:

Using a Directory Let's say that you're interested in getting a general idea of the information available on volcanoes and that your time is somewhat limited. In this case, you might visit one or more directories to get an idea of the kinds of links available for your topic.

Using a Search Engine If you are looking for very specific information, you might want to start with a search engine. Use the keywords you identified in Step 4 to develop your search query. The trick is to try several combinations of keywords, using

(*Continued*)

terms from all three columns in your keyword chart. Possible keyword combinations include: *volcanoes* and *dangers; volcanoes* and *photographs* and *erupt; volcanoes* and *National Park Service;* and *volcanoes* and *predict* and *eruption.* Visit Refining Your Search for more tips.

Using Bookmarked Sites If, somewhere throughout your web travels, you've bookmarked a reliable science web site or one focusing specifically on volcanoes, try starting there. Explore its information and (if possible) visit the other sites it links to.

Remember: There's no one *right* way to conduct research on the web. Just be sure to start with a strategy and experiment with different search tools to get the best results.

Not getting the results you expected from a search engine? One simple step you can take is to make changes to your search query. Try using different modifiers, phrases, or synonyms to make your query even more specific.

Then I have them put this into practice by conducting an internet scavenger hunt. He is one I have done with my elementary students:

Internet Scavenger Hunt

Practice using a variety of search tools by completing the Scavenger Hunt below. Look for each answer by using the website provided after each question.

1. What are the date of birth and birthplace of Edgar Allan Poe?

   Search: www.google.com

   _____

2. In what year did Ireland gain its independence from Britain?

   Search: www.yahoo.com

   _____

3. What movie won the Academy Award for Best Picture in 1976?

   Search: http://awardsdatabase.oscars.org/

   _____

(Continued)

4. What is the tallest building in the world? How tall (in feet) is it?

Search: www.wikipedia.com

_____

Now choose your own search engines and answer the following questions:

5. Who is the "father of modern art"?

_____

6. What is the definition of the following math terms: range, median, and mode?

1.
2.
3.

7. How many days in a year on the planet Neptune?

_____

I also have an Enrichment With the Gifted Guy that shows students how to properly do an internet search. It can be accessed at https://youtu.be/YUcCII5nGHU.

What Impact It Will Have on Your Teaching/ Classroom

This will have a big impact on the way you teach because you will not be the one doing the teaching. Handing over the reigns to the students can be an uncomfortable position for some teachers, but if you have a good structure in place and checkpoints to make sure students are not way off base, you can be assured that learning will occur. This might mean using group contracts to keep them on task. These group contracts allow students to state their learning objectives and then make sure they address them. Here is an example of a contract:

Project Contract

Student Name: _____

Project Name: _____

Learning Objectives [3 to 5]:

-
-
-
-
-

Other Skills Learned:
-
-
-
-
-

Overall Goal of Project: _____

_____

_____

Product of Project: _____

_____

Categories for Public Evaluation: _____

_____

(include public)

Student Signature: _____

Teacher Signature: _____

Parent(s) Signature: _____

The purpose of this contract is to keep students focused on their main objective. This starts with the essential question, which is what you want students to get from the lesson. This can be created by you or together as a class, but every group will have the same essential question(s). It allows the group to lay out its learning outcomes while at the same time setting a goal. Both of these are specific to this particular group. Goals might be something like:

- ◆ Everything is turned in on time
- ◆ Each person contributes something to the final product
- ◆ We get an A on the lesson

Then every time you sit down with this group, you have them pull out this contract and together you go over the essential question of the entire lesson as well as the learning objectives to make sure they are on the right path. I always end by asking them how they are doing toward working on their group goal. This reflection allows groups to figure out ways to improve their working relationship as well as consider what their role in the group is and whether they are contributing the appropriate amount or not.

How Much Work It Will Require of You to Successfully Execute It

The beautiful part about such enrichment is that the students are doing the work for you. Your job now is to manage the classroom and provide supports and resources where they are needed. It's like having 30 student-teachers in your classroom. This means setting up conferences with the student or groups to gather information about their progress. There are typically three times of conferences:

- ◆ Status Conference
  - • Basically maintenance reviews, checking in with the group and making sure they are where they need to be in regard to their deadlines. This involves the teacher and students sitting down to determine where exactly the group is in their timeline of the work.
- ◆ Process Conference
  - • What have we done well so far?
  - • What do we want to improve for the future?
- ◆ Product Conference
  - • Do they know their parts, their materials, their equipment, and so forth.
  - • Does the planned lesson teach the learning objectives they set out to teach?
  - • Will your assessment be able to determine mastery?

You would schedule the appropriate conference with the group depending on where they are in their preparation.

Strategy 17

Higher-Level Questioning

Todd Talk Explaining the Strategy
https://youtu.be/UdO2E4OPF5E [4]

Overview of the Strategy

In my educational opinion, the single greatest thing you can do to enrich your gifted students is to ask the right questions; specifically, higher-level ones. Why is this? Because it is these questions that engage the brain and challenge the thinking of students. That begs the question of when do you ask higher-level questions. Here are some places where you can ask higher-order thinking (HOT) questions:

- Bell ringer
- Exit ticket
- Homework
- Worksheets
- Essential questions/Learning objectives
- Activities
- Reflection/Journal
- Assessments
- Discussion
- Student greetings

If you haven't figured it out yet, you can add HOT questions almost anywhere. It is fairly easy to do. You just have to be purposeful about it and plan accordingly.

The first thing to help you in your journey is recognizing what a higher-level question looks like. There are lots of ways to categorize questions from Costa's Three Levels of Questions, to Webb's Depth of Knowledge, or Fusco's Questioning Strategies. However, the one I believe does the best job when working with gifted students is Bloom's Taxonomy. This is how Bloom's breaks questioning down:

DOI: 10.4324/9781003238577-17

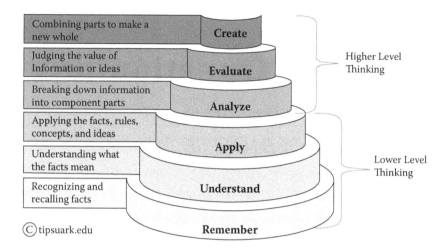

My reason for liking Bloom's is that most of the aforementioned systems only has higher-level thinking at the very top. For Bloom's, it offers three different kinds of higher-level questions you can ask: analyze, evaluate, and create. It gives you more tools to use in your toolbox of higher level thinking questions.

The other thing I really like about Bloom's is that most times the verbs provide you with a clue as to what level of thinking the question is at.

Remembering	choose, define, find, how, identify, label, list, locate, name, omit, recall, recognize, select, show, spell, tell, what, when, where, which, who, why
Understanding	add, compare, describe, distinguish, explain, express, extend, illustrate, outline, paraphrase, relate, rephrase, summarize, translate, understand
Applying	answer, apply, build, choose, conduct, construct, demonstrate, develop, experiment with, illustrate, interview, make use of, model, organize, plan, present, produce, respond, solve
Analyzing	analyze, assumption, categorize, classify, compare and contrast, conclusion, deduce, discover, dissect, distinguish, edit, examine, explain, function, infer, inspect, motive, reason, test for, validate
Evaluating	appraise, assess, award, conclude, criticize, debate, defend, determine, disprove, evaluate, give opinion, interpret, justify, judge, influence, prioritize, prove, recommend, support, verify
Creating	build, change, combine, compile, compose, construct, create, design, develop, discuss, estimate, formulate, hypothesize, imagine, integrate, invent, make up, modify, originate, organize, plan, predict, propose, rearrange, revise, suppose, theorize

You can look at a question and depending on the verb used in it, you can determine at what level of thinking it is asking of students. For example,

Describe the setting of the moor in *The Hound of the Baskerville*.

This falls under the category of understanding. A student would read this description in the book and then summarize or repeat back what the text directly said. However, if you asked this question:

Infer why Arthur Conan Doyle would have used the moor as a setting to heighten the suspense.

Here students would have to dig a little deeper by analyzing. They would have to look at the dangers the moor is described as having in the text and how Doyle could use the fact that one could sink in the moor if they step in the wrong place to increase the suspense of the book. This is not explicitly stated but is a logical inference that could be made if thinking about it.

What It Looks Like in the Classroom

One of the biggest challenges of using higher-level questioning is recognizing when you aren't. You need to be more aware of the questions you are asking of students. If you had asked me in the first five years of teaching how many higher-level questions I asked in my classroom, I would have said a lot. After all, I always had essay questions on my assessments, we had classroom discussions over controversial topics, and students seemed to be challenged. Then I took a hard look at the sorts of questions I was asking using a graphic organizer such as this:

Ques.	CS	MC	SA	ER	GR				Higher Level Ques.		
						Remb.	Under.	Appl.	Anal.	Eval.	Creat.
1.											
2.											
3.											
4.											
5.											
6.											
7.											
8.											
9.											
10.											

What I came to discover was that I was asking a lot of application questions, but rarely was going above this. Surely I was doing a better job during discussions:

Level of Bloom's	How Many Times It Is Being Asked in Discussion
Remembering	
Understanding	
Applying	
Analyzing	
Evaluating	
Creating	

I would use this graphic organizer to gather data for my discussions. I would put little tally marks for the level of the question each time I verbally asked one in class. Strike two. I was certainly asking questions, but they were mostly remembering or understanding. Very rarely was I asking students to analyze or evaluate. This gathering of data opened my eyes that I needed to be more cognizant of the questions being asked.

Once you are aware of how much you are truly using higher-level questioning in your classroom, then you have to be deliberate about creating them both in written form and in the questions you verbally ask. You can use stems such as these to ensure that the questions you are asking are at the higher thinking levels of Blooms:

Analyzing
♦ What is fact, what is opinion?
♦ What conclusions can you draw about…?
♦ What is the relationship between…?
♦ How is _____ related to…?
♦ Can you distinguish between…?
♦ What ideas support the fact that…?
♦ What evidence can you find…?
♦ What inferences can you make about…?
♦ What do you see as other possible outcomes?
♦ What assumptions do you make about…?

Evaluating
♦ Do you believe…?
♦ What do you think about…?
♦ Find the errors.
♦ How would you have handled…?
♦ Judge the value of….
♦ Do you think _____ is a good thing or a bad thing?
♦ How would you feel if…?

- ◆ Can you defend your position about...?
- ◆ What would happen if...?
- ◆ What changes to _____ would you recommend?

Creating
- ◆ What would happen if...?
- ◆ What advice would you give...?
- ◆ What changes would you make to...?
- ◆ Can you give an explanation for...?
- ◆ Can you see a possible solution to...
- ◆ If you had access to all resources, how would you deal with...?
- ◆ Propose an alternative.
- ◆ How else would you...?
- ◆ Can you design _____ to _____.
- ◆ How many ways can you...?

Keep in mind, I am not suggesting that all of the questions you ask be of the higher-level variety. You need the lower-level questions as building blocks in the learning. A student must understand and be able to apply something before they can begin to create and evaluate. What I am saying is you need to maintain a balance in your classroom, trying to make 50% of all of the questions you ask in whatever form higher level. That means writing assessments with this in mind, scaffolding lower-level questions into higher-level ones. It means rethinking your worksheets and homework so you are not only asking students for simple recall and comprehension, but are pushing their thinking. Here is a Todd Talk on how you can make your homework, worksheets, and tests more rigorous using higher-level questions https://youtu.be/_JRUFQQ8-Tg.

When having discussions with students, don't just look for facts or that students have read what you asked them to. How are you expanding their thinking and causing them to look at it in a new way, bringing their own ideas as well? Some things to consider when you are scripting questions for your discussions:

- ◆ Am I asking an open or closed question?
- ◆ What type of response do I expect from students? Is the question phrased in a way to allow this to happen?
- ◆ Do I have a good mix of questions on the full range of Bloom's taxonomy?
- ◆ What will I do if students answer differently than I expect? What is plan B?
- ◆ Do I have dead-end questions? These are questions that stop the progress of the discussion because there is nowhere to go with them.
- ◆ Do I have enough questions to sustain the discussion? You should always have more questions than you are going to actually use.

It even goes as far as the questions you ask students when they come into your classroom. Instead of asking them how they are doing or some other cursory question that will only receive a cursory response, challenge them to think about their response a little with questions such as these:

- What was the stupidest thing you heard someone say today?
- What is really exciting you this week?
- What new ideas are giving you energy lately?
- If you could have any superpower, what would if be and why?
- What is one thing we could do right now to make this day/week even better?

You want to create a culture in your classroom where higher-level questioning just becomes part of the norm. When students come through the doors to your classroom, they know they might be challenged with a question and are up to that task. You cannot just decree this culture, it must be created by the teacher. Some things you can do to help with this are:

- Create a higher-level thinking question for each lesson.
- Require ALL students to answer the question.
- Require students to defend answers by offering probing or follow-up questions.
- Differentiate questions as appropriate. What you ask one student you might rephrase when asking another, depending on their understanding.
- Promote examination of new and different perspectives. Students should be willing to question themselves and you must do the same.

Where to Find Resources

One resource that was especially helpful to me when first venturing into getting better at higher-level questioning was what was called a Bloom's flipchart. On this were the verbs for each level of Bloom's along with some question stems to refer to when writing your own. I would have this by my side when writing my assessments and classwork, and would carrying it with me when leading a discussion, flipping to different levels to help me form the next question. You can purchase these flip charts for a few bucks or if you are cheap like me, you can make your own. If you go to www.thegiftedguy.com/prof-development under Tools for Higher-Level Question, you will find all of the resources you might need to create your own flipchart.

In addition to the tutorial at the beginning of this chapter, I have created the following Todd Talks to assist you in asking higher-level questions:

- Bloom's Taxonomy https://youtu.be/2mHspZ_PKYw
- Raising the rigor https://youtu.be/fqZXvc91u40
- Teaching to the level of the standard https://youtu.be/APuBeL-qRjI
- Probing or follow-up questions https://youtu.be/gYW913YIyQc

I have some templates that will help you in writing higher-level questions. They can be found at https://www.thegiftedguy.com/prof-development under the heading Tools for Higher-Level Questioning. Some of the resources are as follows:

◆ How Does Your Questioning Behavior Rate
◆ Verbs for Bloom's Levels of Thinking
◆ Giant List of Blooms
◆ Question Stems
◆ ELA/Math HOT Stems
◆ Self-Editing Assessments Graphic Organizer
◆ Higher-Level Questioning Presentation
◆ Creating a Culture of Higher Level Thinking

I have also written an entire book on this topic for Prufrock titled *Promoting Rigor Through Higher-Level Questioning: Practical Strategies for Developing Students' Critical Thinking*. This book expands on a lot of the ideas contained in this chapter and goes intogreater detail on how to create this culture in your classroom.

Another resource to consider is the content standards themselves. Many times they are written with a specific level of thinking in mind. For example, take this Common Core ELA standard:

CCSS.ELA-LITERACY.WHST.6-8.1.B

Support claim(s) with logical reasoning and relevant, accurate data and evidence that demonstrate an understanding of the topic or text, using credible sources.

In order for students to show mastery of this content standard, they are going to have to do some analyzing. Write questions that will allow students to be able to do this. Here is a Common Core math content standard:

CCSS.MATH.CONTENT.6.EE.A.2

Write, read, and evaluate expressions in which letters stand for numbers.

Many teachers might stop at writing and reading expressions in which letters stand for numbers. Unfortunately if these are the questions you are asking of your students, they are not mastering the standard at the level it was intended. You need to make sure you are asking questions where students get the opportunity to evaluate expressions in which letters stand for numbers.

With gifted students however, you might not want to stop at the level the standard is asking for. You would want to go above and beyond this, asking students to create when the standard only calls for an understanding, or to analyze something that is only being asked to be applied.

What Impact It Will Have on Your Teaching/Classroom

If done properly, this strategy can have a huge impact on your teaching/classroom. Every question asked in the classroom from your assessments, to your homework, to your worksheets, to your oral questions will all become stronger and require students to think a bit deeper. This will transform you classroom so the impact on your teaching will be high, a 4. This strategy causes you to think about your day-to-day practices and can change the way you go about asking questions and determining mastery of your students.

It will most likely also require you to make some changes to the way you do things in your classroom. It could be as small as revising a few questions here and there, to completely rethinking the way you create your assessments.

How Much Work It Will Require of You to Successfully Execute It

This strategy will require a lot of reflection on your part. Reflection on what you have done in the past, reflection on what you might need to do to make changes, reflection on how you can continue to grow in this area. Admitting you may not have been doing something as well as you thought can sometimes be a difficult thing to do, but a necessary one if we are to become better teachers. Some reflection questions you might consider:

♦ After looking at your assessments, worksheets, homework, and the verbal questioning you do in your class, are you surprised at your questioning behavior? Where do you see room for improvement?
♦ How aware are you of how you construct any written questions you use not only on assessments but in day-to-day activities?
♦ What does a safe questioning environment look like in your classroom? Are there things you could be doing to encourage more of this risk-taking amongst students? What would your ideal questioning classroom look like?
♦ How willing are you to make changes in your questions in order to make it more rigorous for students and thus challenging them?
♦ If there was something you could change in your classroom tomorrow when it comes to questions, where would be the first place you would do so?

Inquiry Learning

Todd Talk Explaining the Strategy
https://youtu.be/JfLo13Grx5M [5]

Overview of the Strategy

Inquiry-based learning (IBL) is a teaching strategy where instead of the teacher presenting facts, there is a question, problem, or scenario posed that students consider. They then identify and research items in order to come up with a solution, expanding their knowledge. Students are learning what they have discovered, not what the teacher has given them. The learning is student-centered and active, meaning students are more likely to be engaged.

IBL goes through these steps:

Ask: Using prior knowledge and understanding, have students pose an essential question or questions concerning a given topic.

Investigate: Students then collect evidence to either prove or disprove the essential question.

Create: From this information, students are able to create new knowledge.

DOI: 10.4324/9781003238577-18

Discuss: Students then present their findings, discussing and debating the results. Reflect: The metacognition of thinking about what the student learned from the activity.

If a teacher wants students to learn about nouns, he or she could ask them what they know and don't know. Students start discussing that they already know a noun is a person, place, or thing, but someone poses what is a person, place, or thing? Typically it is something you can touch. Students *ask* the essential question of, is a noun always a person place or thing or are there exceptions? They *investigate* this, researching whether there are exceptions to the rule. Someone stumbles upon the fact that a noun can be an idea or abstract too. Then students generate examples of when a noun is an idea:

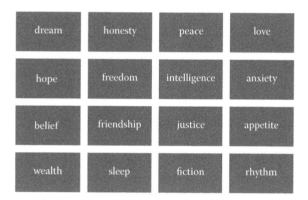

dream	honesty	peace	love
hope	freedom	intelligence	anxiety
belief	friendship	justice	appetite
wealth	sleep	fiction	rhythm

While *creating* the list, students *discuss* and debate whether these are indeed nouns as well as why they are not a person, place, or thing. Once the list is finished, they *reflect* on the fact that there are exceptions in the English language rules. They might generate more exceptions such as:

♦   i before e except after c (glacier, weird);
♦   verb is always an action (hear, seem, own);
♦   e at the end of the word is silent (recipe, resume); or
♦   sentence always ends in punctuation (lists).

This might lead to further learning and discussion, starting the cycle over again.

What It Looks Like in the Classroom

If you walked into a classroom that was using IBL, what would it look like? One thing is for sure, it will look very different than your traditional classroom. Instead of the teacher leading the discussion or driving the lesson, the students are in the driver's seat. Here is what an inquiry-based lesson might look like in a math class.

In order to generate ideas, the teacher goes to the board and writes the term "decimals". Then the teacher asks the class this question. "What do you know about decimals that you find interesting, how do you see them in the real world, or what would you like to learn about in more detail"? Students begin to generate ideas, shouting them out so fast the teacher can barely keep up writing them: "money", "statistics", "measurement". The sharing of these terms sparks other ones from students such as specific types of statistics or measurement and what it looks like when making change.

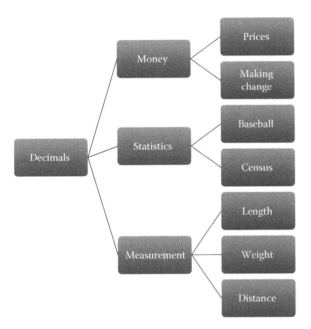

The important thing is you are letting the students drive the conversation with no idea being out of bounds. For instance, students might get into some non-academic terms such as:

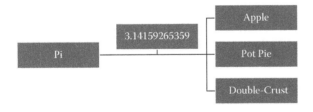

You can let them go down this road for a little bit, only bringing them back if they get completely off task and lose sight of the topic. You could also find a way to bring this back around to the topic:

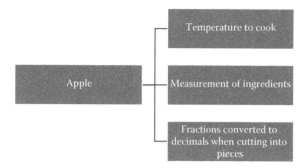

The important thing is to provide the space for students to explore. Many times they will take the learning someplace you would not have imagined.

If students do not have any prior knowledge, you might peak their interest by showing a video that shows the topic of inquiry. For example, if you are wanting to talk about the topic of deforestation, you might show this video on the destruction of the Amazon Rain Forest:

https://www.youtube.com/watch?v=SAZAKPUQMw0

From this, students can write down questions of their own. These might be:

◆ Why does the government allow deforestation to occur in the Amazon?
◆ What happens when so many trees are cut down?
◆ Is it too late?
◆ Can it be stopped?

These questions then drive their learning further as they seek to find answers to them.

Where to Find Resources

One of the challenges of inquiry learning can be corralling the ideas of the students into usable learning. You can use graphic organizers to help funnel these thoughts like the one here:

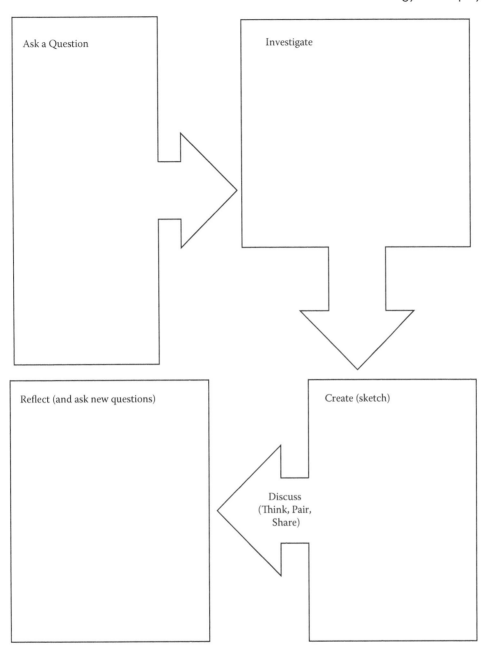

Ask a Question

Investigate

Reflect (and ask new questions)

Create (sketch)

Discuss
(Think, Pair,
Share)

Or thoughts could be organized using an I-Chart (inquiry chart):

Topic					
	Question 1	**Question 2**	**Question 3**	**Other Info.**	**New Questions**
Source 1					
Source 2					
Source 3					
Summary					

This allows gifted students with their thousands of ideas to get them into a usable format.

You do not have to provide the resources because it is now the students' responsibility to find information and apply it where necessary. You do need to provide the space for them to do this as well as the technology. You might have to teach certain skills such as research, information synthesis, how to collaborate, respectfully debating, and others to ensure that the learning is able to be done by the students. You can conduct surveys with students to determine what they are already comfortable with and fill in the blanks for those they are not.

Students might also need some suggestions for products that demonstrate their mastery. If you could use a choice board to help with this such as this:

Audio	Visual	Verbal	Written
Film	Exhibition	Interview	Journal
Play	Model	Journal	Letter
Poem	PowerPoint	Lesson	Newspaper
Song	Art	Oral defense	Short story
Musical	Venn diagram	Presentation	Graphic novel
Podcast	Chart	Press conference	Brochure
Instrumental	Animated movie	Role playing	Webpage
Jukebox	Map	Demonstration	Riddles/Puzzles
Storytelling	Mosaic	Testimony	Story cube
Meditation	Advertisement	Skit	Essay/Research paper

I like using this with my students because you can mix and match. I might ask a student who is particularly shy to do one from the verbal column to try and get him or her out of his or her shell while providing him or her with the choice of how he or she does so. Or if a student is a strong writer, he or she can choose something in that category to stick with their strengths.

What Impact It Will Have on Your Teaching/ Classroom

This is a definite 5. Inquiry is a very nontraditional way of learning but by being student-led it means students are using their considerable talents and skills to drive the learning. They are born with this innate curiosity and as educators we should be harnessing this. Inquiry learning is a strategy for doing so. Your classroom will seem very unorganized at first, something that is difficult for many teachers to endure, but as you hand over more and more of the control of the learning, you will begin to see how deep students will take some of the topics that you were barely going to touch on. It is an excellent strategy for working with gifted minds.

How Much Work It Will Require of You to Successfully Execute It

This is one of those strategies that if done correctly will involve very little work on your part in preparing the lesson. Instead, students would go through each of the steps, making decisions for themselves and where the learning is going to go. Because of this, the role of the teacher is more of a facilitator who guides the students, often with questions that will expand the thought process rather than answers that will stifle it. Most of the work for the teacher comes in walking around the room and engaging in conversations with students, inquiring what they are doing, how they are doing it, and why they are doing it.

Depending on how many times your students have done inquiry learning, you might have to lead them a little bit at first, laying breadcrumbs for them to follow, until eventually you no longer place the breadcrumbs and instead allow them to find their own way. Ideally you can simply mention a topic, and let students unpack it, discuss what they already know about it, determine what it is they still need to learn about it, and then figure out how to show this.

The four levels of involvement of the teacher in inquiry-learning look like this on a spectrum:

Most teacher control   Least teacher control

Structure inquiry   Controlled inquiry   Guided inquiry   Free Inquiry

Structured inquiry: Here the students follow the lead of the teacher and everyone is following along at the same pace and same topic as one big class. The teacher is mostly responsible for where the inquiry goes.

Controlled inquiry: Students work individually to answer the questions rather than as a whole, but the teacher is still the one choosing the topics and identifying the resources students will use.

Guided inquiry: The teacher chooses the topics but it is up to the students to decide what the product is going to be.

Free inquiry: Here the teacher's role is greatly diminished and it is mostly up to the students to choose their topics, the resources they will use to answer the questions, and what the outcome of this inquiry is going to be (MacKenzie, 2017).

My suggestion is that you start with structured and as you and the students get more comfortable with inquiry learning, you can begin to move down the spectrum, doing controlled inquiry until you finally reach free inquiry. If you start with free inquiry, this might be tough for you and your students because they have probably never been given this much control over their learning.

Project-Based Learning

Todd Talk Explaining the Strategy
https://youtu.be/lr_clQhXuKY [5]

Overview of the Strategy

There is a large difference between doing projects and project-based learning (PBL). The major difference is when they occur as well as the amount of new learning that takes place. Projects usually come at the end of a unit and are a review of what the student learned previously, allowing them to apply the skills or content. There is not much new learning taking place. PBL takes place during the unit and is *the* method students are using to learn the new material. To view a Todd Talk on the differences between projects and PBL go to https://youtu.be/D0zmS4tBIwA.

PBL is a way to teach and learn. By having students engaged in PBL in your class, you are teaching them to become independent learners. No longer are you leading the day-to-day lessons. Students are learning on their own, at the pace they are capable of. That is why PBL is a great strategy to use with gifted students. It allows them to take the learning as far as they can while at the same time, teaching them valuable executive function skills that some gifted students struggle with such as given here:

♦ Paying attention
♦ Organizing, planning, and prioritizing
♦ Starting tasks and staying focused on them through to completion
♦ Self-monitoring (working independently)

What It Looks Like in the Classroom

The PBL classroom looks a lot different than your traditional classroom. PBL is student-led, meaning students are making a lot of the decisions of where their learning goes. There would of course be input from the teacher as to what is going to be learned, but how it is

DOI: 10.4324/9781003238577-19

learned, at what depth, what product will be used to demonstrate mastery, and how to manage one's time would be determined by the students.

Here is a project that I did in my classroom:

Create a New Monopoly

For the product of the economic unit, students will create a board game that puts into practice economic terms.

Terms should include:

◆ Productive resources
◆ Entrepreneurship
◆ Trade-offs
◆ Specialization
◆ Absolute advantage
◆ Comparative advantage
◆ Interdependent
◆ Supply and demand
◆ Scarcity
◆ Private/public sector

The game must have:

◆ Marketable name
◆ All game pieces and/or board needed
◆ Clear set of rules of how to play and win
◆ Container for the game

The purpose of the game should be one of two things:

1. Person playing it would learn about the economic concepts.
2. Game uses all of the economic concepts to accomplish a goal of winning.

Students will have two weeks to learn the terms and create their board game. On the day the game is due students, will trade games and play them to help them review for the unit.

Besides giving them this syllabus, students were merely given a due date when they had to have their game ready. We did play the game of monopoly at the beginning of the project to demonstrate and discuss how it puts economic concepts into practice and models the different elements of a board game including pieces, a game board, and directions, but there was little if any teacher-led instruction. How students used their two weeks was completely up to them. I had suggestions of how they should pace themselves, but ulti-mately they determined when and how long they would be working on a part based upon their own skills and how quickly they got it. They had to find the definitions of the terms and gain a good enough understanding of it to be able to put it into practice in the game. They were the ones directing their learning. I would provide them with this rubric to give them the expectations, but how deep and involved their game was left completely up to them.

Create a New Monopoly Game

Students: _____   Game: _____

Overall	Content	Game	Group work
Excellent	• Covers all ten economic terms in depth. • By the end of the game someone who is playing it would have learned a great deal about economics.	• Has a complete and clear set of instructions with the game. • All game pieces are present and add to the understanding of economics. • Game board and/or appearance of the game is very professional, looks like something you'd buy in the store.	• Group is on task and makes great use of class time to complete game. • Works together well, everyone pull his/her weight.
Good	• Covers all ten economic terms but only at a surface level. • By the end of the game someone who is playing would learn something about economics but not a clear understanding.	• Has a set of instructions but some parts are confusing or certain steps skipped. • All of the game pieces are there but do not add anything to the understanding of economics. • Game board and/or appearance is nicely done although some parts could look more professional.	• Group is on task most of the time but gets distracted and does not take full advantage of the class time given to complete game. • Works together well for the most part but at times relies too much on one or more members.
Needs Improvement	• Does not cover all ten economic terms. • By the end of the game not sure that someone who is playing would learn anything about economics or what is learned is trivial.	• Missing instructions or they don't give you and idea of how to play the game. • Missing some game pieces or not enough of them to actually play an entire game. • Game board and/or appearance is sloppy in many places and distracts from the overall experience of the game.	• Group is often off task and wastes much of the class time given to complete game. • One or more group members did a majority of the work while the others did not pull his/her weight.

Some students who only gained a basic understanding of the concepts had simple games. Those who gained a deeper understanding of it had much more complex games. This end product allowed them to display what level of understanding each group reached. Notice in addition to evaluating the economic concepts they needed to learn, I also was looking at their ability to collaborate with others, a valuable 21st-century skill. The rubric allowed me to evaluate both content and skills.

My role during this project was to wander around the room, looking at what students were doing, addressing any questions student have, monitoring to make sure groups were working effectively, but watching them learning on their own. I learned a lot through these observations including their strengths and weaknesses, and most important, how best to challenge them.

This was how every one of my units was set up, with students learning the content through the process of working on their project. Sometimes I would have them work in groups, sometimes with a partner, and sometimes by themselves. We were able to cover from the beginning of time thru the Renaissance using PBL as well as other concepts such as economics and geography. I was always concerned I wasn't going to have enough time to fit everything in if I wasn't constantly feeding my students information, but found that PBL not only allowed for me to expose students to all that was required, they gained a much more enduring understanding of it as evidenced by their year-end achievement scores. I felt like I wasn't wasting class time giving them more space to learn, and more importantly they seemed as though I wasn't wasting their time.

Where to Find Resources

PBL is not something you should enter into lightly. It is very different than most school and thus switching over to that mindset can be challenging. I would definitely recommend doing your homework on what exactly PBL looks like and more crucial, what it would look like in your classroom. PBL Works has a lot of workshops to help folks get started in PBL and there are several books on the subject. I have written a book titled *Project-Based Learning for Gifted Students, 2nd* that explains in much further detail how to enter into the PBL world. I also have several books that contain fully developed projects in them complete with project descriptions, rubrics, and lesson plans for executing it. These can be accessed at www.thegiftedguy.com/books.

You can find a lot of ready-made projects out there whether it be on the internet or through books, but you want to make sure they aren't summative projects but rather formative ones. What I mean by this is a summative project is one that you do after the learning has taken place. You learned something and now you are going to put it into practice by completing this project. A formative project means that by doing it, you are learning the material as you are working on it. It is a process of learning. The project itself takes the place of worksheets, activities, sets of problems, and homework. It is the main driving force behind the learning.

If you do decide to create your own projects, I have a section on my professional development page https://www.thegiftedguy.com/prof-development called Tools for PBL that has blank templates for a syllabus, calendar, and rubric as well as an example of a project menu in addition to how to develop an objective rubric.

What Impact It Will Have on Your Teaching/ Classroom

It transforms it. PBL is a complete 180 to the traditional classroom. In the traditional classroom the teacher is leading the learning, while in PBL the students lead the way. It will also teach your students to become independent learners. Because they have to use skills such as listed here:

◆ time management
◆ collaboration
◆ research skills
◆ problem solving
◆ written or oral communication depending on the product
◆ perseverance
◆ initiative

Students become life-long learners and can use these real-world skills whenever they need them.

You can certainly use PBL in your classroom here and there, but to fully gain the experience and benefits of it you should make it the main pedagogy in your classroom. My last ten years in the classroom were spent in a PBL environment, and students left my class with much more important skills than any content could provide. It was the teaching of these 21st-century skills that gave me and my students the confidence that they would be successful no matter where their learning took them.

I also spend a good couple of weeks at the beginning of the year training students how to work in groups successfully. While PBL can be done with individual kids, it is really built for collaboration. And yet what we often do is throw kids together in a group and hope for the best. I found this out the hard way when having students work on a timeline project together at the beginning of the year without any preparation for what it means to work in a group. Students were bickering, some were in tears, I had parents calling or emailing to tell me how unfair their student thought the group was acting, it was a complete disaster. After that, I thought it worth the two weeks spending getting them trained if it meant for a smoother collaboration the rest of the year. We did things such as:

◆ Identifying strengths they bring to groups
◆ Developing norms
◆ Establishing different roles in the group
◆ What good group dynamics looks like and when it is going south
◆ Coping mechanisms when things aren't going well
◆ Introducing them to reflection, self and peer evaluations

I found that by being purposeful about this training, groups were much more effective and could better produce work together that was better than they could have done by themselves. I have some Todd Talks on how to do this group training that you can view:

◆ Student Collaboration https://youtu.be/Bv0B1cStL8o
◆ Roles in Group Work https://youtu.be/VxYx0Dzqios
◆ Creating Group Norms https://youtu.be/JzQo7Pt8mBw
◆ Student Self/Peer Evaluations https://youtu.be/x1VzZrNt7tU

How Much Work It Will Require of You to Successfully Execute It

PBL requires a lot of work up front. You have to (1) create the project. You can certainly take someone else's project and use it for your classroom, but if you decide to create your own projects, you can tailor them to meet the needs of your students. I generally followed these steps when creating my own projects:

1. Define the problem: This is the standard, essential question, or learning objective(s) you want students to have gained by the end of the project.
2. Develop solution options: This is either choosing the product that students will create in order to display their mastery of the skills, or allowing students to choose for themselves.

You also have to (2) determine how you are going to evaluate for mastery. This typically means developing a rubric that clearly shows students what they will have to do in order to be successful on the project.

3. Plan the project – Once you have made the first two decisions, you need to plot out what this is going to look like and how long it will take. You can do this on a calendar. You must also determine how you are going to assess what students have learned. This usually takes the form of an objectively written rubric.
4. Execute the plan – This is communicating the project to the stakeholders. This is first and foremost the students, but also includes parents, team members, and admin-istration. The form this would take would be a syllabus, calendar, and rubric that is provided and explained to students at the start of the project.

Once you have begun the project, the amount of work you have to do is much less than a traditional teacher. You are no longer in front of the class a good majority of the time, delving out information and ways to apply it. Instead, students are independently working on their projects. Your job shifts from teacher to that of manager, which involves you going around the classroom and having conversations with students. These might be conversations about their progress, it might be conversations about the approach they are taking, it might be conversations challenging their thinking, or it might be challenges about themselves, getting the chance to learn about your students. During this time you are executing step 5:

5. Monitor and control progress – This involves you providing the resources students might need, making sure they are on task, checking in with them occasionally to see how they are progressing, but generally staying out of their way to allow them to do the work they must do to complete the project.

Once everything has been completed and the product has been turned in and assessed, there is one additional step to PBL that typically is not done in a traditional classroom.

6. Close project – This involves students reflecting on the project, looking at such things as what went well, what could have been better, what did they learn about the problem, or what did they learn about themselves. This reflection can be teacher-directed using writing prompts or protocols, or once students get in the habit of it, just like the rest of PBL students can do this themselves.

Differentiated Centers

Todd Talk Explaining the Strategy
https://youtu.be/P7rnPcJbcCs [5]

Overview of the Strategy

Differentiated centers are centers spread throughout the room that students go to and engage in varying activities based upon the level they are ready to learn at. It involves students moving through centers, either given a certain allotment of time, or at their own pace. The teacher is not providing direct instruction but rather is coordinating the centers and checking in with students to determine their progress. This allows the teacher to cover a lot of different skills in a single class, as well as students to progress at a pace and level they are able to handle.

What It Looks Like in the Classroom

A teacher is wanting students to learn about heat transfer. Depending on the student, they may be at different places in their understanding of this. If a student has already covered the basic definition of the different types of heat transfer, he or she probably has a better understanding than most, while someone who does not even recognize the terms might have to start from the beginning. If you have the same exact activity for all students, you are either leaving kids behind or boring them because they already know it and know it well. You might end up teaching students that fall in the middle, but that is only a handful of your class.

In differentiated centers, students are presented with three tasks:

a. Do you know what convection, conduction, and radiation are in relation to heat transfer? If not, look up these terms and write down definitions.
b. If you have a general understanding of what convection, conduction, and radiation are, could you explain them to someone who does not know? How would you do that?

DOI: 10.4324/9781003238577-20

c. If you are very familiar with convection, conduction, and radiation, provide multiple examples of how these are used and to what purpose. Use specific examples from your own life.

At the center are some articles, some of which just go over the definition of what the three types of heat transfer are, and another set of examples of the types being used in the real world. Students also have their Chromebooks as a resource. One student reads the articles and writes down in a notebook the basic definitions of each of the types of heat. Another creates a video of their explanation of each of the types of heat. A third decides to create a Google Slideshow that shows photos of various devices and explains the types of heat they are using. Each student is getting the learning objective of knowing the three types of heat transfer, but some are getting the basics while others are going more in-depth based on their prior understanding.

You the teacher are not assigning these students to these different tasks, but rather students are determining for themselves which ones they will attempt. If a student thinks they should be doing task B, but then gets a little way into it and discovers that he does not know as much as he thought, he can always move to task A, build a basic understanding, and then attempt task B again if she so chooses. Or if a student choose task A, and while in the middle of it realizes he has already learned this in another year and thus skips over to task B which will enable him to take this basic understanding he already possesses to the next level.

This group of students moves on to another center in the lesson, only this one is about the difference between potential and kinetic energy:

a. What are the definitions of potential and kinetic energy?
b. What is the difference between kinetic and potential energy?
c. How do position or chemical energy affect potential energy, and how does motion affect kinetic?

As you can see, there are layers being added to each choice.

When students moved to another center, the understanding might change. The students who knew a lot about heat might not know anything about kinetic and potential energy and thus get the basic definitions, while the one who did not know much about heat can tell the difference between potential and kinetic.

Every center in the science class would be about the topic of heat such as:

♦ Heat transfer
♦ Determining temperature
♦ Thermodynamics
♦ Conservation

And at every one of these centers are multiple activities for students to choose from that will enable them to learn at the level they are capable of. This is differentiation at its finest. These would not necessarily be done in a single day, but be left up for several days to allows students enough time to work through them at their own pace. If some students finish early, there could be bonus opportunities or chances to dig even deeper into the topic.

You could set up your centers to scaffold into higher, deeper-level thinking. In social studies class, you label your centers as such:

G – Gain an understanding
O – Observe how to apply this skill
A – Analyze how you might use this skill in your own life
D – Delve deeper into ways this skill might be used

The topic is economics. At each center there is an activity that builds upon the next:

G – Students will identify key economic terms such as:

- ◆ Supply and demand
- ◆ Specialization
- ◆ Interdependence
- ◆ Scarcity
- ◆ Surplus

O – Take a collectable item such as comic books, coins, baseball cards, NFTs, sports memorabilia, or something of your own choosing. Explain how the price of these items is determined by all of the economic terms you learned.
A – Think about how you might use these economic terms in your own life. Where would you see these in action? Write this in a diary or journal entry in a Google Doc.
D – To go deeper and use these concepts in a real-world situation, as a class, we will play the trading game.

The Trading Game

Each group is going to represent a different country.

1. United States
2. Britain
3. France
4. Spain
5. China
6. Brazil
   o You'll get an envelope with the goods you already have.
   o There are ten total goods as well as currency in the form of Copper, Silver, and Gold.

1. Cow
2. Corn
3. Wheat
4. Wool
5. Fish
6. Coffee
7. Tobacco
8. Silk
9. Rice
10. Chocolate
    - Everyone will be in need of some goods
    - The object of the game is to sell your surplus and then buy the items you need to survive.
    - At the end of all the trading, there is going to be a couple of countries that will not get everything they need and fall into economic depression.

Here is what you need to succeed:

Two cow
Two corn
Two wheat
Two wool
Two fish
One coffee
One tobacco
One silk
One rice
One chocolate

Rules of game

- You can only sell good card for money card.
- You can only buy good card with money card.
- Trading must take place at the trading center (center of the room).
- You will complete three rounds of trading in which you have to get all the items you need.
- A different person must be used for each round of trading.

If you would like a complete version of the Trading Game, including the playing pieces, further directions, and reflection, you can download it for free at www.thegiftedguy.com/resources under The Trading Game.

You can even get creative and have centers that specifically deal with your subject area. For ELA, the teacher could set up READ centers.

R – Reinforce Writing Skills
Students

♦ respond to Article of the Week prompts;
♦ complete various writing tasks to demonstrate understanding of the three main types of writing; and
♦ use a variety of editing techniques to enhance their writing.

E – Expand Your Vocabulary
Students

♦ are exposed to Latin and Greek stems;
♦ compile an interactive notebook;
♦ interact with words in context;
♦ use computer-based study aids or game based study activities; and
♦ are self-paced.

A – Achieve New Knowledge
Students

♦ watch a teacher created video or slideshow to learn new grammar or language content;
♦ take notes in their Language Interactive Notebook; and
♦ demonstrate knowledge in a variety of ways.

D – Demonstrate Thinking Skills
Students

♦ participate in a teacher-led lesson;
♦ learn reading standards;
♦ interact as a whole group and in small group situations; and
♦ complete short-term activities to make connections between the reading standard and the in-class reading material

Students are given their READ sheets (developed by Erin Muck) to guide them through the centers:

This READ sheet and ALL activities are due the morning of Wednesday, September 12, 2018!!!

READ

Name _____

9/10/18-9/11/18		Materials	Directions	Quick Check (Complete AFTER the task!)
R	**Reinforce Reading and Writing Skills** **CCSS.ELARI.7.1.** **I can cite several pieces of textual evidence to support analysis of what the text says explicitly as well as inferences drawn from the text.**	Pencil Pouch Chromebook Colored Pencils	☐ **Article of the Week-** **Text Evidence-Explicit and Implicit** • Follow the link on Google Classroom to a Prezi over explicit and implicit text evidence. • Complete the notes (found in the station bin). • Show Mrs. Muck your notes. • Read the story and answer the questions that follow.	Turn the story questions into the class tray.
E	**Extend Your Vocabulary** **CCSS.ELAL.7.4.B.** **I can use common, gradeappropriate Greek or Latin affixes and roots as clues to the meaning of words.**	Vocab INB Pencil Pouch Chromebook Scissors Glue Colored Pencils	☐ **Vocabulary-** Each person is now on the self-paced portion of vocabulary. It is important to dedicate time to vocabulary every READ rotationto stay on pace to finish by the end of the nine weeks!	**Check in with Mrs. Muck after each step is completed.**
A	**Acquire New Knowledge** **CCSS.ELAL.7.1.** **I can demonstrate command of the conventions of standard English grammar and usage when writing or speaking.**	Language INB Pencil Pouch Chromebook Earbuds Scissors Glue	☐ **Noun Functions in a Sentence-** • Use the slideshow on Google Classroom to learn about the different noun functions in a sentence. • Read the slideshow for directions on how to cut and glue the flaps into your LANGUAGE interactive notebook. • Glue and write the information onto PAGE 6. • Show your notes to Mrs. Muck.	**The noun mind map is due on Friday!** **Complete the following questions.** 1. What type of noun is the word ability as it is used in the following sentence? Superdad has the amazing ability to nap at any time during the day. a. singular concrete noun b. plural abstract noun c. singular abstract noun d. plural concrete noun 2. What type of noun is the word World Science Instituteas it is used in the following sentence? Dr. Fist was kicked out of the World Science Institute for conducting forbidden experiments. a. plural proper noun b. singular common noun c. plural common noun d. singular proper noun
D	**Demonstrate Thinking Skills**	Pencil Pouch	☐ **I Am Malala-** **Lesson with Mrs. Muck : Theme over Genres** • **Listen to Malala's speech to the United Nations in 2013** • **Read and annotate** • **Discussion**	**What is one quote from the speech that stood out to you while reading or listening to it? Why?** _____ _____ _____ _____ _____ _____ _____ _____

You will notice in all of these examples students are being pushed to a higher level of thinking, which is why they are good to use with gifted students.

What Impact It Will Have on Your Teaching/ Classroom

If done correctly, it will have a large impact on your classroom. These centers can be used for one day, a couple of days a week, or the entire week. They could be done occasionally or become a part of the classroom culture. I had math and ELA teachers who taught for our gifted magnet program who did these differentiated learning centers the entire year. Students had to be shown how the system worked, but once that was done, students were able to be completely independent. This did take a tremendous amount of preparation on the part of the teachers, but once the centers had been developed, they could be used the following year with just a few adjustments based on the previous year's experiences. When I would walk in, it looked very much like a different classroom in a good way. Students were spread around the room, deciding which activities they would do as well as how they would demonstrate mastery of learning. When I would go up to students and ask them what they were doing, nearly every one was able to explain to me where they were in the process and more importantly, what they were supposed to be learning. The teachers sat at a table in the middle of the room and did check-ins with students or provided feedback on work that had been turned in from the last cycle.

How Much Work It Will Require of You to Successfully Execute It

The role of the teacher is different from what it would be if you were teaching in a traditional classroom. There would be a lot of work upfront in creating the various centers and providing the resources, but once students are doing the learning, your role becomes more of the manager, making sure everything is running smoothly, keeping track of time, and replenishing resources if need be.

You can also be one of the centers in your stations. I have seen teachers who have seats at the U-shaped table and groups of students would sit and work with her. This allowed her to check-in with students to see where they were and also to provide some direct instruction if need be.

Conclusion – How an Expanded Toolbox Can Lead to You Being a Better Teacher

The profession of teaching is a lot more difficult than most people think (not a secret to you I am sure). One of the major reasons is because there is no one right way to teach students, no one size fits all (another secret, this book is chock full of them). What works with some students does not with others even if the students are seemingly similar in ability level and interest. In order to deal with this, we keep many tools in our toolbox so that when we have a specific task to do, we can pull out the correct tool. There are certain strategies that work best in certain settings or situations. It is important to have many to choose from so that students are getting the most from your classroom. If you just have one tool you are not going to be able to do many things, just like if you only have a hammer in your real toolbox, you can certainly pound nails in, but cutting wood or unscrewing a screw would be difficult if not impossible. That is why it is important to have several different tools in your toolbox; the more tools you possess, the better you can apply the correct one to the correct job.

You have hopefully looked at a few of the strategies presented in this book, you might have looked at just one, you might have looked at over a dozen. What I encourage you to do is to try some of these that put you outside of your comfort zone as a teacher.

I have been in education for 25 years, and yet I have found myself in recent years trying new strategies for teaching. When I was offered the chance to teach students in China, I wound up in a culture that was very different from my own, teaching a class that I had never taught before, using curriculum that was not created by myself. Needless to say, at the end of the seven days in a row of teaching 8-hour days, I knew things had not been perfect, but I had learned a great deal. When, like most teachers, COVID caused me to have to adapt to virtual learning, I had to figure out a way to deliver engaging learning to students in a platform I was unfamiliar with. Having used Depth and Complexity only on a minimum scale, next year I will be teaching a cognitive class for third graders that centers around the thinking platform.

I enjoy trying new ways to teach, and learning along with the kids because that is what makes teaching still interesting to me. If I expect my students to learn by taking risks and going outside of their comfort zone, then that is what I need to expect of myself. As a colleague of mine said to me in my first year of teaching; you can either teach for 30 years, or you can teach one year 30 times. I could certainly do what I have always done, but that is not what is best for me as a teacher nor is it best for kids.

DOI: 10.4324/9781003238577-102

References

Brookhouser, Kevin (2015). *The 20time Project*: *How Educators Can Launch Google's Formula for Future-ready Innovation*. CreateSpace Independent Publishing.

Kingore, Bertie (2003). High achiever, gifted learner, creative thinker. *Understanding Our Gifted*. Retrieved from https://www.coloradogifted.org/wp-content/uploads/Bertie-Kingore-High-Achiever-Gifted-Creative.pdf

MacKenzie, Trevor (2016). *Dive into Inquiry: Amplify Learning and Empower Student Voice*. EdTech Team Press.

MacKenzie, Trevor. (2017). *Do You Have an Inquiry Classroom?*. Ed Tech Team Press, June 12, Retrieved from https://trevmackenzie.wordpress.com/2017/06/12/do-you-have-an-inquiry-classroom/

National Science Foundation (2016). National Science Board Science and Engineering Standards. Retrieved from https://www.nsf.gov/statistics/2016/nsb20161/uploads/1/nsb20161.pdf

Randazzo, Laura. "Facing failure". *Lauren Randazzo – Solutions for the Secondary Classroom*. Retrieved from https://laurarandazzo.com/2019/02/23/facing-failure/

Stanley, Todd (2014). *Performance-Based Assessment for 21st-Century Skills*. Prufrock Press, Waco, TX.

Printed in the USA
CPSIA information can be obtained
at www.ICGtesting.com
CBHW081017040524
8055CB00028B/483